GOLDEN ODDLIES

'The humour of Mr Paul Jennings is English, and his method entirely his own ... he has Chesterton's habit of seeing familiar things as though he had suddenly noticed them for the first time.'

So wrote Beachcomber (J. B. Morton), introducing the first 'Oddly' book. Over thirty years later Jennings's prose is as hilarious to modern readers, his style as engaging, as in 1949 when he became *The Observer*'s first humour columnist.

Gathered in this volume is a whole range of Jennings pieces. There are his musings on the things that happen to him – such as hearing the voice at the end of the British Rail telephone answer '"Euston Sleepers"' ('I couldn't have been more awed if it had said "Delphic Oracle, at your service" or "Vestal Virgins, good morning"'); his study of the inner meanings of place names (for example, 'I feel a bit wembley today'); his demonstrations that Things are against Men, including the famous satirical piece on 'Resistentialism'; and many other well-loved Oddlies.

GOLDEN ODDLIES

The Cream of the 'Oddly Enough' Column
Paul Jennings

A Methuen Humour Classic

This selection first published in Great Britain by
Methuen London Ltd
11 New Fetter Lane, London EC4P 4EE

This selection has been taken from the following titles: *Oddly Enough*
(1950) published by Reinhardt & Evans, and *Even Oddlier* (1952), *Oddly
Bodlikins* (1953), *Next to Oddliness* (1955), *Model Oddlies* (1956), *Gladly
Oddly* (1958), *Idly Oddly* (1959), *I Said Oddly, Diddle I?* (1961), *Oodles
of Oddlies* (1963) and *Oddly at Lib* (1965) all published by Max Reinhardt.

All the pieces in this book originally appeared in *The Observer*,
with these exceptions:
'Hitting the Nail on the Thumb' and 'Advice to Husbands': *House and
Garden*; 'Harley Street': *Family Doctor*; 'A Diversity of Doctors':
originally a pamphlet sent to doctors by Payncoil, but now owned by the
Beecham Research Laboratories Ltd; 'Just a Few Friends': *Housewife*;
'Report on Resistentialism': based on an article originally published in
the *Spectator*, although the piece as it now is appeared in *Town &
Country* (USA)

ISBN 0 413 53890 7

Made and printed in Great Britain by
Richard Clay (The Chaucer Press) Ltd,
Bungay, Suffolk
Filmset in Monophoto Imprint by
Northumberland Press Ltd, Gateshead

CONTENTS

v

CONTENTS

INTRODUCTION?

But haven't we met before?

Dear Reader – dear, I hope, *buyer* of this book, although of course there is now this Public Lending Right scheme which means I get a farthing or something even if you've only just got it out of the library – I suppose it depends whether you were born before about 1970. You can't have been born much after that – unless you are actually reading this in 2000 (and that's what books are *for*, after all. Fancy causing your thoughts to get, by means of these little black marks on paper, into another person's head after you are dead – and whilst I don't want to be morbid, I don't feel absolutely certain of seeing 2000. Even better, fancy making that person *laugh* after you are dead. This particular book is coming out in a series with other authors who *are* dead. One of them, A. P. Herbert, wrote pieces which made me laugh, years after he was dead, every time I read them in the process of copying, proof-reading and eventually seeing them in an anthology I did).

But suppose you were born around 1970 and have bought this book pretty soon after its publication. After all, you have to be twelve or thirteen or something to like this kind of stuff (and after that of course I hope you will go on liking it more and more at least till you reach eighty-two, which is what I'll be if I *do* make 2000). And I promise the nearest I shall come to boasting about this book, apart from admitting that I am (a) proud that over thirty years ago the *Spectator* said I was '... one of those ... nearly extinct human beings, a thoroughly *English* humorist' (my italics) and (b) delighted that this book is coming out while I am still not extinct, is to say well, I did get a letter from a twelve-year-old boy asking where he could get a previous collection, long out of print.

Everybody knows that Swift said 'Good God, what a genius I had when I wrote that book!' even if they can't remember which book it was (nor could I till I just looked it up in the *Oxford Book of Quotations*, it was *Tale of a Tub*), and perhaps fewer know that Belloc titled the Introduction to *The Path to Rome* simply 'Praise of this Book'; and I hope everybody will know that quoting things like that is not an indication that the quoter has any grandiose ideas that he should be on the same bookshelf or even in the same room as those great men, but is a consequence of the extreme difficulty of writing, before becoming extinct, an Introduction to a Collection of Collections.

The fact is, Dear Reader, *I don't know how old you are.* You may well have been born (like me) about fifty years before 1970, in which case you may (or may not, according to what Sunday paper you took) have read the fortnightly pieces in the paper and not bought the Collections. You may have bought the Collections (which had names like *Oddly Enough, Oddly Bodlikins, Next to Oddliness, I said Oddly, Diddle I?*) and never seen the paper in which the pieces appeared. You may have read the pieces *and*, God bless you, have bought the Collections. You may have bought the Collection made from the Collections after five or six of them had appeared (there have been thirteen and, not counting this one, there is very likely to be a fourteenth; I told you, I'm not extinct). This book, which has some things from Collections which appeared after that Collection of Collections, and could therefore be described as a Collection of Collections from Collections, may be your very first sight of the stuff. Or you may be like that twelve-year-old boy whose parents had one of the Collections and lent it irretrievably to someone, although even if you were you could have got to forty or something by now. For instance, if you were twelve when the first Collection came out, in 1951, you could now be forty-four.

To paraphrase T. S. Eliot, I have measured out my life in

fortnights, except for a brief period when I appeared in one magazine every week. And some of those fortnights were a good time ago.

So you see what I mean about its being difficult. We frivolous fellows have no illusions about our place, if any, in the great corpus of Writing. I remember once seeing a pamphlet about Modern American Literature by whatever is the American equivalent of the British Council, no doubt the Office of Something and Something. There were great slabs about Theodore Dreiser and E. Hemingway and T. Wolfe and of course Scott Fitzgerald (although there are at least a few smiles in *him*), but that great man Thurber was a four-line footnote, and the almost equally great Benchley wasn't in at all.

In other words, if you are lucky enough to be even a foot-note to start with, is there any point in writing footnotes to a footnote? To take one example, you dear multi-aged readers, there are bound to be those among you who are young enough never to have heard of the Button B, referred to in the first paragraph of the piece called 'Far Speaking' (p. 13). Ought I to have this footnote saying it was a courteous appendage, long since vanished, of the public telephone, which you pressed if the voice at the other end was not the one you wanted, *and you got your money back*; it didn't start going *poo-poo-poo* the moment they'd lifted the phone at the other end, the way it does now, so that you can't tell. Indeed, ought I to go on and say that this money was two good old pennies, of which there were twelve in a shilling (now known as 5p) and 240 in a pound?

Ought I, in the piece called 'A Diversity of Doctors' (p. 126) to say that when it first appeared, to write that The Friend Doctor was 'Husband of girl you know. Very gay, tells wonderful stories ..., etc.' did not arouse the sniggers it would today; it was before the beautiful word 'gay' had been stolen by Drears Lib? Well I have now, of course; but as I said, you see what I mean.

You get footnotes, you are only a hair's breadth away from starting to go on about Humour, what it is. Well, neither I nor anyone else can tell you what it is. But I know what it should *do*, if it's any good, and whenever it was written. Make you laugh.

One last footnote then. In 'Drop In for Billiards' (p. 95) it would be insulting for me to tell you that the Viscount was an aircraft, or aeroplane as we used to call them. It's obvious. But there must be some of you who don't know how proud B.E.A. (British European Airways. O God!) were of this first great turbo-prop with its four engines. I daresay there are still a few of them, kept going by cannibalized spare parts, flying on obscure internal routes in China, because we did sell them a few. But then it was new, exciting. And I just hope that's the difference between humour and aircraft, between humour and almost anything. Real laughter is (oh, how one hopes it is!) timeless, ageless, eternal. The funniest thing I ever saw in my life was a clown routine in the old Bertram Mills circus, when I was ten, which involved two men, a step ladder, and about a hundred buckets of water, and the obvious intention of each clown of pouring water down the other's trousers. I was sick with laughter. Last year I saw exactly the same thing in a circus in France and it was just the same. In the end the audience were turning round to stare at *me*. . . .

I can't hope to rival that. But if any of this stuff, and never mind the duodecimal currency or anything else, touches that sacred nerve and makes you laugh, well God bless you, and may none of us ever become extinct. I say this even if you have only borrowed this book from a friend who got it from the library. If you bought it, God bless you even more. If you laugh, you really are Dear Reader, and I really am Yours Sincerely

PAUL JENNINGS

PSYCHOTYPING

It always gives me quite a shock when I see typists typing and realize that they *aren't looking at the keys*. It seems incredible. I can remember the top row, qwertyuiop, because that is a kind of word; you can pronounce it. It would be quite a good onomatopoeic word for corkscrew, *qwe–rt* being the squeaky noise of the cork turning round and *yui*–OP being it coming out. But asdfghjkl, although fairly memorable, is too confusing, with 'a' and 's' so arbitrarily added to the alphabetical sequence. And as for zxcvbnm – I don't see how anybody could remember that.

Some time ago I asked one of these no-look typists how she did it. She said they began by typing that thing about the quick brown fox, slowly. Well, I tried it slowly and I got this remarkable poem:

> th quoci
> The quick briwn fox jiumoec the quock bobrow
> the quock bo
> the qi
> the quicj brown hox ji ji jumoef over the lazu fod
> the quoci
> thr quo
> the quick brown fox jumpeffed over the lazu llazy fdodfdoh
>   dodof f dof doh doh dog.

I realized straight away that I have remarkable gifts as a typewriter medium. These ordinary typists, by a rigid mechanical discipline, have imposed their conscious will on the machine, making it write dreary orders for spangeing irons, and thursling rods, and copper and silk stone grummets. But the typewriter takes me straight into the collective unconscious of the West. Jung says somewhere that the nightmare, the fire-breathing horse that symbolized terror for preindustrial man, is being replaced by locomotives or great black machines out of control. So, too, the typewriter replaces the planchette, the sybil, or the inspired idiot as the mouthpiece of these verbal race memories. We do not know yet what the *quock bobrow*, or even the *quock bo*, is. The typewriter throws up these disturbing concepts for our consideration and then goes off into a counter-melody in the scat-singing idiom (*ji ji jumoef*); then there is a return to this *quoc* motif, or archetype. The last line produces a splendid verb, *jumpeff* – so much stronger than mere 'jump'. It suggests the fox (or *hox*) sailing insolently over the *lazu fdodfdoh*, going '*pff*' contemptuously as it does so. Yet this marvellous extension and exploration of language is all done in the medium of a popular song, like Edith Sitwell's earlier verse. I should like to hear Danny Kaye sing that last line.

It is fairly clear, however, that the typewriter is trying to come through with some basic message about the *quoci*. A little patient work by a trained analyst would soon straighten it out. But it is not always so simple. The typewriter taps such a rich, teeming world that several attempts often disclose no unity to the layman. Consider, for instance, these two versions of a well-known poem:

> matu laf a lyttle lamv
> id gleece was qgite as sbei
> abd evertwhere that maty wabt
> that lamh was stee to ho.
>
> maty gas a lyyrrlr lavm pamb lanm
>   labm lamn lamh ba blast
> utd forrcr aa waa whire as svie
> abd everytgwee ygar maty webt
> yhat la, j waa sure yo go
>
> kank lamj nub b b b lamn lamb
> 575757575

How *European* this is! What lyrical variations are called

up by the tender associations of 'little' – the charming Anglo-Saxon *lyttle*, the April, Chaucerian bird-song of *lyyrrlr*! Observe the Romanian *sbei*, the Germanic *stee to ho* (compare Siegfried, at the end of Act One, singing to Tolstoy's disgust, *Heiho, Heiho! Aha! Oho! Aha! Heiaho!* You could easily add, *stee to ho!*). And then we come right into our own dialects with *yo go*, which, of course, is pure Birmingham.

The curious line at the end looks at first like the sort of thing that comes through on a teleprinter when they are testing it. But when we look carefully we see that 575757575 is an expression of ecstasy at the appearance of the word 'lamb' which has suddenly come out right. We can appreciate the rational beauties of ordinary speech all the more after we have had these glimpses of the dark creative chaos from which it has emerged – the fascinating world of the gleece and the kank.

In this vast field which I have opened up there is great need for a proper, regularized, statistical method. There must be thousands of typewriter mediums like myself, and if our findings could be collated I am sure it would widen the whole field of modern psychology (there need be no conflict with existing science; you will notice the significant reference to *id* above). But the psychologists had better hurry up, while there still remain poople who xannot type.

HOW TO SPIEL HALMA

The other day, when I was in one of those shops that sell old lithographs and Prospects, and boot-trees, and tiled pictures, and 1920-ish faded yellow dresses, and old copies of the *Saturday Evening Post*, and little lead shoes, and clocks of green marble shaped like Birmingham Town Hall, I found a dusty old box containing a game of Halma. In German.

I bought it, because the instructions looked so fascinating. I am not what you would call fluent in German. I know just enough for me to bumble along in a half-understanding daze, feeling comfortably that by knowing just a few more words I could speak it like a native. I desist from actually learning these few more words because I know that in fact this would be a dreary process extending over several years while I found out about things like *Schicksal* and *Empfindsamkeit*; and because I also know that during the first half of this period the pleasant sense of comprehension which I feel now would diminish rather than increase.

My friend Harblow doesn't really know any more German than I do. But he is never content to allow a German sentence to remain merely a matter for pleasant speculation. As soon as he discovered my Halma, nothing would please him but that we should evolve a theory of the game from the extremely explicit-looking set of instructions on the lid of the box, and actually play.

Neither of us had played Halma before, but Harblow pointed out that the board seemed straightforward enough, like a chessboard seen through a telescope the wrong way

4

round, and with zigzag enclosures in each corner. 'Now, let's try the first paragraph,' said Harblow briskly, and he read on:

'*An diesem Spiel können sich 2 bis 4 Personen beteiligen, von denen jede eine Farbe wâhlt, und damit, wenn 2 Personen spielen, einin großen Hof mit 19 Steinen, wenn 4 Personen spielen einen kleinen Hof mit 13 Steinen besetzt.*'

The only difficult words here seemed to be *beteiligen* and *wählt* (I just happened to know that *Farbe* is 'colour'). Our (mainly my) translation ran thus:

At this Game 2 or 4 Persons can betake themselves and each of these wears a Colour and damn it, when 2 Persons play, a big House with 19 Stones, when 4 Persons play, he besets a little House with 13 stones.

It was clear enough for me. It conjured up a pleasant picture of these Persons wearing their Colours and heraldically besetting each other's Houses like something in a Book of Hours. 'Damn it' I took to be an idiomatic way of saying that the real way to play this Game is with 4 Persons. Of course, if you must, you can play with 2 Persons, but damn it, it's a pretty poor show. Harblow, however, insisted that *damit* means 'with that' or 'therewith', so I allowed this, to pacify him; although it didn't seem to make any more sense.

The next sentence said: 'The Players now try so quickly as possible with their Stones to beset the House of the Against-man [*Gegner*] and he is the self-same Winner [*Gewinner*] who the first *gelingt*.' Even Harblow had no theory for *gelingt*, so we went on to the main paragraph, a magnificent jumble of instructions of which we could not translate any particular sentence except one; but the general sense was that you got to the Against-man's House by the process of *überspringen* or overspringing, as in draughts. The sentence we did understand was *Es kann auf diese Weise eine ganze Reihe von Steinen übersprungen werden* – in this Way it can a whole Row of Stones be oversprung.

We started to play, with 19 Stones (damn it), and we moved one at a time to beset each other's Houses until our forces met in the *Mittel* (Middle) of the *Feld* (Field). Suddenly

Harblow, by a most curious progression involving horizontal, vertical, *and* diagonal moves, oversprang five of my stones and arrived behind my zigzag thing. To my protests at the obvious irregularity of this he replied: 'Well, it says here that you can move *auch seitwärts oder rückwärts,*' as if that settled it.

'Well, what does that mean?' I said.

'Either sideways or – well, *rückwärts.* I am sure "forwards" is *vorwärts,* and you couldn't want to move backwards, so *rückwärts* must be one of these untranslatable words for the silly way a knight moves in chess.'

'What way is that?'

'Er – two forwards and one sideways.'

'I'm sure it's two sideways and one forwards.' (We don't know much about chess either.)

In the end we agreed that you could overspring a Stone that was next to you in *any* direction. When I jumped over some of my own as well as Harblow's Stones to beset his House he objected, but I pointed out to him that it was possible *über eigene und fremde Steine fortzuspringen* – over own and strange Stones to jump strongly. I had him there.

As the game progressed, if you can call it that, it began to dawn on us that we were not clear what was meant exactly by *besetting.* At the beginning we had agreed that when you oversprang the Against-man's Stone you did not remove it from the board, as in draughts, because if you did this neither *Spieler* would have any Stones left to beset the Against-man's House *with.* On the other hand, if there were not some system of being sent back to base how could this sentence be construed?

> *der Gegner muss natürlich wiederum danach trachten, diesen Stein womöglich in dem eigenen Hof des Spielers einzuschliessen.*

The obvious meaning of this was that the Against-man must naturally again after that treat, this Stone how possibly in the own House of the Player to shut in. It obviously implied arriving before the Against-man's House with pretty large forces, a thing quite impossible to achieve by either party, however cunning, if being oversprung meant the loss of a Stone every time. And another thing that rather militated against anybody shutting anybody else in was the fact that it was perfectly easy for both *Spielers* to evacuate their Houses completely, long before the Against-man arrived anywhere near the scene.

So the game rather petered out. Harblow's view, for which he can offer no proof, is that the rules we evolved would work all right with 4 Persons. But, of course, the difficulty is to find 2 other Persons whose knowledge of German is exactly the same as our own.

WARE, WYE, WATFORD

I never know whether to be surprised or not when I am told that foreigners find English extraordinarily difficult. On the one hand it is less rational, more 'given', than, say, French or Spanish, which have the air of being mental constructions; and it is more manifold, more European, than, say, German. On the other hand there is surely, about most English words an ultimate rightness which ought to strike everyone, including foreigners, as the final perfection reached in man's art of naming. I don't mean the obvious, satisfying onomatopoeia of words such as *bang, dribble, snivel, splotch* (all my French dictionary can do for splotch is *grosse tache* – I ask you!); for there is a more subtle, allusive onomatopoeia in words which have nothing to do with actual sound: *sausage, elation, leaf, humdrum*; if boredom made an actual noise, that's what it *would* sound like; *hum, drum, hum, drum*.

Our island is the home of a magical aptness, the ancient tussocky fields are the nearest approach, so far, to that ever-new Garden of Eden in which, as Mr W. H. Auden recently reminded us, Adam's first task was to give names to the creatures. If anyone doubts this, let him consider the very names of our towns. For they not only describe places. They carry wonderful overtones, they seem to have been drawn from some huge, carelessly profuse stock of primal meaning, to have come out of the very bag from which Adam got his names. Let me illustrate with a few examples from this vast English treasury of subconscious meaning:

babbacombe n. An idle or nonsensical rumour. 'It's just a lot of b.'
barnstaple n. Mainstay, keystone. 'Mrs Thomas is the b. of our committee.'

8

bawtry adj. Used of windy and rainy cold weather. 'A b. day.'

beccles n. Ailment of sheep, cf., the Staggers, the Twitches, Quarter-ill, the Jumps.

bovey tracey adj. Headstrong, wilful. 'None of your b.t. ways here, Miss!'

brasted adj. (colloq.). Term of humorous abuse. 'The b. thing's come unstuck.'

buckfastleigh adv. (arch. and poet.). Manfully. *'Aye, and right buckfastleigh, lad'* (Hardy).

cromer n. A mistake, bungle. 'You made a c. there.'

dunstable adj. (arch.). Possible. *'If 'tis dunstable he'll do't, my lord'* (Shak.).

dungeness n. Uninterestingness. 'A suburb of extraordinary d.'

erith v. (obsol.). Only in third pers., in old proverb 'Man erith, woman morpeth.'

glossop n. Dolt, clot. 'Put it down, you silly g.'

holyhead n. Hangover.

ilkley adj. Having large elbows.

kenilworth n. A trifling or beggarly amount. 'He left her nobbut a kenilworth in his will.'

kettering adj. from v. **ketter** (obsol.). Like the flight of a butterfly.

leek adj. Very cold.

lostwithiel n. Ne'er-do-well.

lowestoft n. A subterranean granary.

lydd adj. Useless, defunct, inactive.

maesteg adv. (Welsh). Musical direction to Welsh choirs to sing *maestoso* but at the same time brightly.

manningtree n. A gallows.

midhurst n. Maturity, fruition. 'His career was in its m.'

morpeth see **erith.**

pershore adv. (arch.). Certainly, for sure. *'Pershore thou'rt damn'd'* (Webster).

priddy adj. Neat.

rickmansworth n. (legal). Ancient nominal rent paid to lord of manor for hay. Always paired, in mortgage documents, with –

stevenage n. (legal). Ancient nominal rent paid to lord of manor for stones.

thirsk n. A desire for vodka.

uttoxeter n. A charlatan, usually a quack doctor.

wembley adj. suffering from a vague *malaise*. 'I feel a bit w. this morning.'

woking pres. part. of v. to woke (obsol.). Day-dreaming.

9

HOUSEHOLD NOISES

The death last week of the founder and chairman of Boddery Household Noises recalls one of the most romantic commercial careers of modern times. In 1923 Alfred Boddery, young and unknown, was joke editor in a small matchbox firm, where his inventive mind was bringing him more frustration than advancement. To many men the job would have been satisfying enough; but in between reading the proofs of his jokes, seeing lawyers about copyright, and running down to the printers, Boddery realized that he was in a 'blind alley' occupation. Whenever he had a really progressive idea, such as that of having interminable serial jokes so that the public would buy his firm's matches to see the ending, the management turned it down.

Boddery used to say in later years that he owed the idea which brought him success to his wife. As he was leaving his house with her one night she went back to switch on the hall light, for she shared with many others the conviction that to burglars this would denote occupation and thus keep them away. When Boddery pointed out that all burglars knew that trick, she laughingly retorted: 'Why don't you invent a trick they don't know?'

He accepted the challenge, and the result was Boddery's original Thumping Machine – in principle a large box with a sounding-board; an interior mechanism caused the four thumping arms to beat against this, so that when the machine was left running in an unoccupied house it conveyed the impression of a constant procession up and down the stairs.

The Thumping Machine was an instant success. But

Boddery laid the foundations of Household Noises not so much by his salesmanship and advertising, excellent though these were, as by the ingenuity with which he always kept one step ahead of the thinking burglar. The latter soon realized that all the bangs and thumps coming from empty houses were unaccompanied by the sound of any human voice. So Boddery brought out his 'Merry Cries' record. The reverse side of this contained the famous One-sided Telephone Conversation. Another popular early line was the Boddery Meal Simulator, a device in which knives, forks, and spoons, suspended from a pulley system, gave a realistic imitation of a hearty meal in progress.

Household Noises rapidly expanded into a major domestic industry. The 1930 advertisement reproduced on the preceding page gives an idea of the remarkable progress made in seven short years.

No scientific development was overlooked by Boddery. Up to his death he was working on new techniques in invisible ray remote control. Last week I was shown over the Household Noises exhibit for this year's Ideal Home Exhibition, in which Boddery had taken a personal interest. As I approached a model house it was wrapped in a ghostly, dark silence. But when I got to within twenty yards and crossed a hidden ray which activated a selenium cell mechanism, the whole place suddenly burst into amazing life. I could have sworn there were three families there. One was singing glees in a front room, and another was having an uproarious party somewhere at the back, a third was playing some mysterious game which involved running up and down the stairs.

A child was doing a bit of fretwork, and someone else was on the telephone. Dogs barked, babies squealed, people played 'The Rustle of Spring' and gargled, and there was someone having a bath. Life was being lived very fully and richly in that house.

It may be long before such luxuries are available to the home market, for, as a Board of Trade spokesman said last week, Boddery's products are in high demand in America and the dollar countries. It is a fitting tribute to this prince of gadgeteers.

FAR SPEAKING

There can be few words more seen and less read than the instructions in public telephone boxes. When we have pulled on three sides and at last found the one that opens, that is our last conscious, willed act; the rest is reflex. We stand on the little square of concrete, in our private world, our whole attention already on our correspondent; we are irritated by any delay, such as the maddeningly unhurried ratchety noise that goes on after we press Button B, as though very leisurely mice were hauling up tiny sacks with a block and tackle. We are certainly in no mood to read instructions.

Hardly anyone would admit to having actually learnt to telephone by reading the instructions from scratch. It is true that, if we are townees, we do read in country kiosks, to our surprise, that all we have to do is to lift the receiver and listen for the operator; and we are mildly interested in the thin little directory containing the numbers of corn chandlers and farriers and the Regent Kinema. But on the home ground our literary attention is at its lowest level – a pity, because the instructions contain the only attempt ever made by Post Office prose writers, as far as I know, at romantic onomatopoeia – 'a high-pitched burr-burr'. It sounds like the scientific definition of a West Country tenor.

This apathy has suddenly been disturbed, however, in a number of London boxes, which have lately blossomed out with instructions in French, German, Italian, and Spanish. They provide a fascinating comparative study, and one's preconceptions about the languages are curiously disturbed; in fact, it is only the Italian which does what one would expect of it, when even a prosaic thing like dialling tone is described as *un trillo basso intermittente*.

The French is disappointing, for where one would expect a kind of marble poetic style it is, in fact, technical where it is not downright illogical. *Prière de s'adresser à l'opératrice en anglais*, it begins. If they can address the operator in English, why can't they read instructions in English, hey? *Décrocher le récepteur à l'orielle et attendre le son musical ... introduire 2 pennies dans le dispositif d'encaissement.* There is admittedly a certain charm in the idea of awaiting the musical sound, as though the box should soon echo with a solemn passacaglia; but we are quickly brought back to technology with the *dispositif d'encaissement*, which sounds like the foundation of a suspension bridge. The correspondent cannot hear you but after the manoeuvre of the button A, we are told with great formality; and *pour rappeler l'opératrice, agiter lentement le crochet commutateur*. Even the stolid English do not talk about the commutatory hook, preferring the fine conceit 'cradle switch'; there is something illogical, too, about the injunction to agitate slowly; one thinks of a kind-hearted Communist who can't help liking his employer.

With the splendid German instructions, however, we step straight into the world of poetry and fairy-tales. The whole apparatus is treated animistically. *Sprechen Sie bitte mit der Fernsprechbeamtin*, they begin, and somehow it couldn't matter less that here also one is invited to *sprechen* to her in English; for the marvellous word, *Fernsprechbeamtin*, has already evoked a placid, fair-haired, semi-mythical Teutonic figure, a kind of Telephone Queen, deep in some German forest – the Far-speaking Beaming One.

As in all fairy tales, there are mysterious commands and taboos to be observed: *dann zwei Pennies in den Automaten werfen* – then throw two Pennies in the Automaton. But *wenn sie die gewünschte Nummer nicht kennen, kein Geld enwerfen:* if you do not know the Wished-for Number, do not throw in any Gold; if you do, the Automaton will probably clank ominously towards you in the thickening twilight, and you will hear behind you *ein schnarrender Laut*, the schnarring noise made by the dragon who also lives in the forest. But somehow Good will triumph. The *Fernsprechbeamtin* will appear at the crucial moment and wave her wand, and you will be joyously reunited with your Wished-for Number, and the *Fernsprechbeamtin* will let you choose three gifts from her palace.

I should choose E to K, L to R, and S to Z to replace three of the four A to D's that are always in my box.

PSYCHOLOGICAL GRADING

All British sociologists will welcome the Report of the Royal Commission for Psychological Grading in Busy Places, published this week for the Ministry of Development and Printing, for it represents the first real official attempt to cope with the problem in modern society of complication-neurosis.

This is a condition which can best be explained to the layman by actual examples. Let us imagine a suburban branch Post Office, with, say, six positions – Stamps, Savings, Money Orders, Position Closed, Pensions and Allowances, and Telegrams. An ordinary customer (in the sociologists' jargon, a neutral counter-unit, or N.C.U.) such as the reader or the writer of this article – a person, therefore, entirely free from complication-neurosis – goes in to buy a book of stamps. He is preceded in the queue by a complication-neurotic who, perhaps, wishes to send a parcel to the Virgin Isles, a possession of the U.S.A. The clerk looks dubious, then calls someone from an inner office with a glass door. They fetch down a big book – the Post Office Guide. They find the section on the Virgin Isles.

'Ah,' murmurs the First Clerk, 'Customs Declaration "A".'

They are not quite sure what this is, so they flip rather aimlessly through the pages until it occurs to Clerk Two to look up 'Customs' in the Index. They find it and Clerk One reads, in an unsure sort of voice, 'Two kinds of customs declaration form are in use, namely an adhesive form to be affixed to the parcel (mainly for Empire use), and a non-adhesive form (for most foreign countries). Two or more copies of the latter form may be required, see pp. 110–209.'

But pp. 110–209 are merely the alphabetical section covering the world's countries, containing the bit about the Virgin Isles where Clerk One started. We are in a vicious circle. But this is only the beginning. When they have finally decided about the Customs, Clerk Two says, 'What's in the parcel?'

'Well, it's a kind of model I made,' says the woman helplessly, 'and a few potatoes.'

'Potatoes, eh?' says Clerk One doubtfully. More page-flicking, then, 'I'm afraid we can't accept it, ma'am.' For under 'Prohibited Articles' it says, for the Virgin Isles:

Letters, cotton seed, cotton and cotton seed products (except oil, manufactured cotton and cotton waste; see below); feathers and skins of wild birds (except ostrich feathers) unless for educational purposes; films or pictorial representations of prize fights; intoxicating liquors; potatoes ...

And so on, while all the normal person or N.C.U. wants is this book of stamps. Not only Post Offices are affected by the spread of complication-neurosis. Evidence submitted to the Commission shows that most of the people who want a simple second-class return to Birmingham in a hurry are preceded by the sort of man who wants to go to an obscure place in the Hebrides. He has voluminous inquiries about sailing tickets and seat places and *insurance*. His ticket, instead of being issued quickly with a metallic thump from a machine, has to be laboriously written out on a duplicate form with long footnotes about 'Messrs MacBrayne's Services'. In a bank, an N.C.U. who merely wishes to cash a cheque for £5, will be preceded by someone with a battered attaché case full of little blue bags full of pennies and complicated company accounts.

The Commission's Report recommends a revolutionary technique of psychological grading, to be tried out experimentally at first in Post Offices.

We are in entire agreement with the experts who have given evidence [it says] that the present division of Post Offices into operational functions is arbitrary and inefficient. We therefore recommend a form of Psychological Grading. In a Six-Position Post Office two of the positions should be labelled 'SIMPLE'. The remaining four should be labelled 'COMPLICATED'. Counter units should be met at the door of the Post Office by a trained psychologist who by the answer given to some such question as 'Good morning sir (or madam); what do you require?' would be able to deduce the degree, if any, of complication-neurosis, and direct the counter-unit accordingly.

I need hardly point out the effect on our social life if the Report is acted upon. Normal people like the reader, or the writer, of this article will be able to pop quickly in and out of the Post Office, even at the busiest times. Complication-neurotics will have a special part of the Post Office all to themselves, screened off with trellis and artificial roses; there will be little tables where they can discuss their problems with fellow-spirits all day long over a cup of Post Office coffee.

The realignment of staff will mean an overall increase in Functionary Time (F.T.) without the corresponding increase in Functionary Units which sociologists previously thought this must involve. The Report, recognizing the existing shortage of psychologists, outlines a scheme for Regional Training Colleges giving a special one-year course. In the Report's concluding words,

the initial expense should soon be repaid, since from Post Offices it is a short step to railway booking offices, banks, and shops, and we may therefore look forward confidently to an efficient rationalization of the whole of our public life.

HITTING THE NAIL ON THE THUMB

The only serious and splendid thing that I have ever made myself is a bookcase. It stands eight feet high and consists of two uprights and seven shelves. I was very proud of it at the time, for it was made with screws. This was none of your slapdash, nailed-together jobs. I bought a chisel (I always have to buy a chisel when I want to chisel something, which is admittedly not often: the old chisel is either lost or so rusty that it looks like some neolithic tool dug up from a bog), I chiselled slots for the shelves, I made three screw holes in each slot. That's forty-two holes. I was at it for a week, just making the holes. I screwed the whole thing together. It gave me a big bruise on the stomach because whenever I screw anything, no matter how much I prepare the whole with a gimlet, when the screw gets half-way in it becomes appallingly stiff and I have to lean my whole body against the screwdriver as I turn it. When I have finished there is a roaring noise in my ears, my wrists ache, and, as I say, there is a bruise on my stomach.

Still, I finished this thing, and very nice it looked. It was made to fit into the space between a wall and a chimney breastwork. But later we moved to a bigger house where there wasn't a space just that size, and I made a terrible discovery about my bookcase. *It won't stand up by itself*. Without a chimney breastwork to hold it up it goes all limp, it creaks over sideways.

I am sure I am not the only man who finds, like this, that there is always some fatal flaw in anything I make myself; and I think where we make the mistake is in trying to do it with wood. I must admit that in my case the inherent awkwardness of wood is intensified by a trauma I suffered at school (everybody explains his shortcomings as being due to childhood shocks these days, so why shouldn't I?). When, one autumn term, we started woodwork at school it was obvious from the start that I was a backward boy in this field; I needed special, understanding, *loving* teaching. I see that now. But the man who taught us was a cross Welshman, and I really believe that he thought I was being clumsy just to spite him. We were placed two to a bench according to our position in form, and this made the Welshman even crosser, because I was second, and therefore at the top bench. 'You must be better at some things than you are at woodwork,' he said, nastily. This was true. Fortunately we did not get marks for woodwork. My benchmate, the top boy, exceeded me not only academically, but also as a carpenter. We'd only been at it for a couple of terms when he was making a marvellous inlaid chessboard, he was allowed to use exotic oriental woods and special glue. His chessboard was in the Exhibition on Prize Day. Most of the form had graduated to making clumsy knife-boxes and pipe-racks, but I never made anything at all because you weren't allowed to until you had mastered a thing called the Mortice and Tenon Joint. Most people managed this after a week or two, but I was still at it after Christmas.

One afternoon, when this damned Mortice, or it may have been the Tenon, had split asunder yet again, I went to ask the Welshman if I could get some more wood from the store. But he seemed very busy helping one of the expert boys with a magically involved box he was making. I didn't want to disturb them, so I just went to the store and took a piece. I was hopelessly drawing lines on this with a set-square when I became aware of a silence, everyone had stopped work. The Welshman was standing behind me.

'I want you all to come here,' he said. 'This boy has disobeyed my orders. He has stolen a piece of wood from the store.' That's what he said, *stolen*. Half of me thought, That's ridiculous, *I* didn't want the dreary wood, the man's crazy.

The other half of me thought, Gosh, yes, he's right, what's the use of being a scholarship boy if I do immoral things like that, *I'm no good*. You see what I mean about a trauma.

But apart from all that, I still think it's aiming pretty high to do things with wood. Wood is only slightly less hard, and therefore slightly more workable, than stone; and no one in his senses would dream of making a stone bookcase. Wood is inexorable, you have to get things right first time, once you have cut or chiselled too much away you can't put it back. I notice that not many of the eminent people one sees photographed Doing It Themselves are working in wood or anything else solid. And the ones that are have such vast workshops, such neat patterns of expensive tools – whole families of chisels, elegant little saws, mysterious power-driven devices – that the thing isn't what *I* call a hobby at all. It's industry. Look at Giles, the cartoonist. Giles welds things. He welds caravans. You get the feeling that if he stopped drawing cartoons tomorrow he could carry on with this welding and Mrs Giles wouldn't notice the difference in the housekeeping money. People from all over East Anglia would bring pieces of metal to Giles and ask him to weld them together.

As a matter of fact, now that my eldest child is four, I have discovered a material in which the deep human urge to make things, which lurks in even me, can be satisfied. I refer to Plasticine. Some of my prehistoric birds are real masterpieces of imagination, even though they won't stand up. Of course, I don't advance that as a serious hobby. If you ask what I *do* do in my spare time, the mad look of the monomaniac will come into my eyes, I shall lead you into a corner, away from all those planes and saws and chisels and needles and paint brushes, and I shall start to talk interminably about Orlando Gibbons, and Weelkes, and Wilbye, and the Authentic Ionian Mode. You haven't got it, you carpenters? Well, my hobby is social, it involves inviting at least three other people – a bass, a contralto, a soprano. We sing madrigals. I won't say how good we are. But I know we're better than that bookcase.

FLAUTISTS FLAUNT AFFLATUS

In the Shaftesbury Avenue district, where in a dusty wind
we struggle back to reality after the bright dream of the
theatre, where shops contain violent blouses and zippy
American clothes, the men's jackets apparently interwoven
with tinfoil (I imagine the wearers clanking and glittering like
bird-scarers as they walk), I have just seen a reminder of a
magic older even than the theatre; for in a music shop there
is a flute, by which stands a card saying

FLUTE. £12. EASILY CONCEALED

Why, although this seems at first sight so strange, does it
also seem so appropriate? It is because the flute is terrible,
mysterious, and primitive. Compared with the flute, other
instruments are courtly and civilized. Sir Malcolm Sargent
tells of a woman whom the sound of a flute always sent into
hysterics. Now that the wild demon of music is snared and
tamed in a great net of counterpoint and mathematics, the
marvellous thin pipings of the flute are a link with older things
– with a fearful liquid ecstasy of melody in the first dawn,
in the first terror of creation.

Of course, even the flute has been tamed a little. *Ah, the
dear Baron has brought his flute*. But underneath those rococo
curlicues of sound there still lies a Maenadic madness. It says
in *Grove* that one of the oldest surviving flutes is a bronze
one found at Armant, Egypt, and when a modern recorder
mouthpiece was put over a facsimile of it 'the Dorian mode
... which formed the basis of the Perfect Immutable System

... was easily obtained'. One sees this experiment in some room at the British Museum – the visitors in the great galleries spellbound, the researchers among their dusty books troubled by beauty, as ancient and immortal melodies steal thinly through the corridors in a music grave, Dorian, perfect, immutable.

The flute had been tamed before 200 BC, by these Dorians; but not completely, nor is it yet. That woman who had hysterics knew what lay underneath, she remembered the God walking by the river, and Krishna playing to the milk-maids.

You have only got to look at people who play the flute. They are much the most mysterious people in the orchestra. We feel we know what string players are like; delicate, dreamy, including women, and with a sprinkling of foreign names – Aronowsky, S., Klein, J., Klumperts, L. They are a counterpoise to the brass – red-faced, jolly, named Parkinson, Cloggett, Greenwood, Tiarks, having a beer in the pub after the concert, reminiscing about the old days at Kneller Hall. But flutes are played by inscrutable-looking men called Rogers or Morris; and we have no picture of them. The orchestra stops banging and roaring, it hangs a quiet curtain of chords for them – and with half-closed eyes they play their warbling solos, the hall dissolves into a sunlit glade ... where did they learn, how do you learn the flute, who teaches it, do these men in the orchestra give lessons, *who are they*?

Of all musicians, flautists are most obviously the ones who know something we don't know. And, just for a second, in this shop window, the veil is lifted, tantalizingly. We catch a glimpse of the flautist; but not, yet, of the flute, for this is concealed – slyly, under a loose coat. The goat-eyed, the devious flute-player moves softly among us, none can see the flute he carries. He walks past unsuspecting doormen, into public assemblies, into restaurants and parties – into churches, even. He nods and smiles, he talks to other people, to us. He does not reveal that he is a flute-player.

For there have been one or two rumours – a pubful of people

in Croydon discovered in a trance, from which they have never emerged; a bus that simply disappeared across fields; a whispered story of platelayers found sobbing in a tunnel, of thin high music vanishing into a cave, of men discovered with a look in their eyes like that of Mole in *The Wind in the Willows*, after he saw Pan. 'For this is the last best gift that the kindly demigod is careful to bestow on those to whom he has revealed himself in their helping: the gift of forgetfulness. Lest the awful remembrance should remain and grow, and overshadow mirth and pleasure, and the great haunting memory should spoil. . . .'

Now the authorities, the upholders of the regular, are beginning to look out for men with flutes. But unperturbed, in his own time, when no one is looking, when there is laughter at the other end of the room – when the lights go out, when the food comes in, when the sermon begins, the flute-player will produce his concealed flute with a deft movement and lift it to his lips – and then, at the first wild note, transfixed, changed for ever, we shall *know*.

BABEL IN THE NURSERY

It is difficult to decide whether translators are heroes or fools. They are surely aware that the Africaans for 'Hamlet, I am thy father's ghost' sounds something like '*Omlet, ek is de pappa spook*', and than an intense French actor, beginning Hamlet's speech to Gertrude with '*mère, mère*', sounds exactly like a sheep. In Denmark the film *King Kong* had to be called *Kong King* because *Kong* means 'King' in Danish. Seeing a book in shops all over France with the title *Autant en emporte le vent*, like a line from Lamartine, I took a long time to realize it was *Gone with the Wind*.

The racial realities of language have become mere intellectual concepts to the translator. He floats over the world in a godlike balloon. The babble of voices under the arches of teeming cities, the infinite variations of uvula and hard palate, the words formed in tribal battles and in tales over the winter hearth, float up to him in a vague, jumbled unity, rich but disembodied, like a distant cooking smell.

Paradoxically, the more a work expresses some special national genius, the more it attracts translators. Until recently I had thought the supreme example of this was *Jabberwocky* done into French, German, and even Latin (*ensis vorpalis persnicuit persnacuitque*). But now I perceive that something even more secret and English has attracted them; the children's books of Beatrix Potter.

Quite apart from their literary style, these have the same 'central' symbolic appeal as Jane Austen. Jemima Puddle-Duck, Mrs Tiggy-Winkle, Ribby, Duchess, and the rest of them live in a transcendentalized English village, where shops

with bottle-glass windows doze in an endless summer afternoon, and nothing changes. No one has heard of foreigners, just
as the Napoleonic Wars are never mentioned in Jane Austen.

The moment even the titles are translated we are very much
aware indeed of foreigners, of Europe. Here are some:

FRENCH:

Sophie Canetang (Jemima Puddle-Duck)
Noisy-Noisette (Squirrel Nutkin)
La Famille Flopsaut (Flopsy Bunnies)
Jeremie Pêche-à-la Ligne (Jeremy Fisher)

DUTCH:

Tom Het Poesje (Tom Kitten)
Jeremias de Hengelaar (Jeremy Fisher)

WELSH:

Hanes Dili Minllyn (Jemima Puddle-Duck)
Hanes Meistress Tigi-Dwt (Mrs Tiggy-Winkle)

ITALIAN:

Il Coniglio Pierino (Peter Rabbit)

SWEDISH:

Sagan Om Pelle Kanin (Peter Rabbit)

GERMAN:

Die Geschichte von Frau Tigge-Winkel
Die Geschichte der Hasenfamilie Plumps (Flopsy Bunnies)

Who *are* these characters, we ask? Well may the inhabitants
of the Potter village peep from behind their dimity curtains
as this babbling procession pours down the quiet street. Here
comes Sophie Canetang, a Stendhal heroine, acutely analys-
ing love with a cavalry officer and a *petit bourgeois* – but
respectable compared with the awful Mauriac Famille Flopsaut, festering with hate, ruining the brilliant son who will
never get to Paris; compared with the gaudy career of Noisy-
Noisette, the Mata Hari of the twenties, as depicted by
Colette, or the Maupassant Pêche-à-la-Ligne, the quiet angler
who pushes his mistress's husband into the trout pool.

Behind these comes Tom Het Poesje, a kind of Dutch Till Eulenspiegel, half jester, half highwayman, a doubtful figure in leather jerkin, plaguing the burghers with rather unfunny practical jokes. Then there is a momentary silence as Jeremias de Hengelaar, the fourteenth-century mystic, shuffles by, pondering on the One.

What on earth does Dili Minllyn, thinking of the April clouds sweeping over her white farmhouse on the green Welsh hill, of the clock ticking on the silent dresser, have to say to Il Coniglio Pierino, the swarthy Sicilian bandit, or to the Nordic hero Pelle Kanin, seen through smoke and fire, howling songs against the northern wind on long-prowed ships?

And who, in this village, is going to be interested in the story of Frau Tigge-Winkel, the widow of a Prussian general who revolutionized something or other in 1874? To say nothing of the Hasenfamilie Plumps I.G., a lesser version of the Krupp dynasty, an endless succession of stern characters extending the family factories in the Ruhr....

Almost it is unfortunate that the children in the village, who have one language and one vision, will not see them.

MONEY BACK

The splendid Georgian façade and the misty sweep of grass-land down to a lake with ornamental bridge belied the near-ness of London, and gave a touch of pathos to the occasional Londoners who passed us, smelling slightly of damp, dark cloth. It was a wet Sunday afternoon in March. There was distant shouting and the thud of soggy footballs. We saw many people with dogs, many without, many alone. Harblow was on leave from the Army, in which he has elected to remain. We felt a little superior to them all. We had something to talk about. We were not merely escaping from bed-sitting-rooms.

As we entered the mansion, which now serves teas, we were talking about the Indian railway station where we had last seen each other. I remembered the teeming families squatting round their brass drinking pots, the glistening brown bodies washing at the pumps; I remembered the curious translation of that British thing, the railway. From its proper Emett milieu of clanking Wolverhampton goods yards and Charles Keene cartoons, to the blinding, indifferent East.

Was it all over? Surely London was still a name for some-thing in the hearts of Englishmen away from England. Surely it wasn't reduced to *this* – this neurosis of damp red brick, those horn-rimmed, close-lipped, pork-pied tabloid readers coughing into their fag-ends in the Tube? Was the great, blind, tragic building mocking us with echoes of a vanished era of expansion and optimism; or was it here and now that the decent English, with their neat schoolchildren, were dreaming of a new order, absorbing even industrialism into a workable way of life?

The tea room was a vast cavern of a place. What would
the French make of this? – a little orchestra, perhaps –
certainly not utility china and a bleak serving table where one
queued for single cups of tea, bread and butter, and railway
cake. A notice said that the caterers solicited orders for
weddings, *balls*, and other functions.

A smaller card said 'Special today, Peach Melba'. Harblow,
who saw nothing tragic in this, put one on his tray – a sad-
looking dish filled with some opaque, orange-coloured substance with a dab of ersatz cream. We sat down in the cavern,
among the children and the dogs and the murmured conversations.

Harblow gingerly took a spoonful of his Peach Melba, and
then said in a confident mess ante-room voice: 'This is the
most hideous stuff I have ever tasted. You try it.'

Rather apathetically, I did so. It certainly tasted awful. I
know aluminium doesn't go rusty; but if it did, that's what
it would taste like. Food should always be organic in origin,
but this had a terrible metallic, *boring* quality – the way a
penny tastes to a child licking it on an endless, boring summer
afternoon. It wasn't just not nice. There was this aggressive,
metallic nastiness. And yet boring. Boring food for another
twenty years. I wanted to rush out to see something living,
even if it was only the damp footballers.

Suddenly I realized with horror that Harblow was going
to protest – *to ask for his money back*. Harblow, I thought
bitterly, is the sort of man who would ask for his money back
at the cinema if the projectionist, the manager, and all the
usherettes were shot dead by bandits two minutes before the
end of the film. I sought wildly for reasons that would
dissuade him, but I could think of nothing that would fend
off the inevitable reply: 'It's the *principle* of the thing.' He
strode up to the counter.... I felt doom all about me.

The manageress was a tired-looking woman with wispy
yellow hair. She looked as though thirteen hours in some
enormous steamy kitchen had drained all the life out of her
(no, no, that was nonsense. They only made tea – and one
pot at a time, at that. But maybe there was a ball tonight).

If she had been a red-faced tyrant: if she had said: 'Well, you don't expect it flown from the South of France for 1s. 6d., do you?' – even if she had given Harblow a Complaint Form to fill up, it wouldn't have been so bad. But she passed the back of her hand worriedly over her forehead. She tasted it:

'Yes,' she said sadly, 'it's not very nice, is it? I don't know, I'm sure. We try to make something nice for people, but it's so hard to get the stuff.'

I knew all about sin when she said that. We were guilty and she was innocent. I thought of her bursting excitedly into her kitchen on Friday afternoon, laden with packets of FRUTO, the Wonder Melba. 'Had to queue two and a half hours,' she would say, breathlessly, 'but look what I've got. Let's give them Peach Melba tomorrow. The little children will love it.' Far into the night she and her associates had worked, mixing the FRUTO and pouring it into hundreds of little glass dishes. Saturday morning would be passed in pleasant anticipation, waiting for the rush. *We try to make something nice.* She would go home tonight, and her husband, an engine driver on half-pay, would knock out his pipe and say, 'Well, dear, how did the Peach Melba go?' She would collapse in his arms. 'Oh, Jim, Jim! They asked for their money back!'

Or maybe there wasn't even a husband. . . .

I had feared a scene, people crowding around, a man in striped jersey taking her side, saying, 'Ho, yus, that's right, Missus,' perhaps elbowing Harblow. But this was much worse than any scene. 'Yes, I suppose you'd better have your money back,' she said listlessly. Harblow had the grace to look ashamed.

I wanted to rush out weeping, to buy the manageress a great big shining motor-car, to blow up London and start again with peasants. Yet so mutable and full of infinite invention are we that when I *did* go through the door I was feeling splendid, sure that the world has much to hear from England yet.

It has. Harblow, without a word, had left a half-crown under his saucer.

QUO VADIS?

In the first half-hour after I have left a theatre I am always convinced that I am going to write a play. It is a curious sensation because I never know what the play is to be about. I just have a general impression, and yet at the same time a very clear one, of dramatic confrontations, of sharp, agonized words cutting into the hearts of a tense audience, without ever knowing what the words actually are.

This doesn't happen at the cinema. There is too much machinery in the way. However moving the film, one will also have seen a newsreel (when I go it always seems to contain a waiters' race in Paris) and a trailer, with little cameos of people being slapped, or surprised in embraces. One remembers all the time that the film is just one more activity of this teeming world.

Yet this week, utterly illogically, I was inspired to write a film, too. I wasn't actually inspired by the film, but by the stills and posters on the muffled way out; for these were to advertise M.G.M.'s *Quo Vadis?* They all looked curiously unreal. I thought of the queue in togas at the studio restaurant, of the obvious gap between modern America and ancient Rome. And it was then that I thought of my film, which will bridge this gap by having the dialogue in Latin.

It is called *Balbi Murus – The Wall of Balbus*. It is the story of a young engineer, Balbus, who has been commissioned by a Government agency, known by its initials S.P.Q.R., to build a wall, that the city may be defended against the Carthaginians. It is the story of his love for Julia (*Balbus amat Juliam*) who is the daughter of Marcellus, a prominent member of the S.P.Q.R. It also tells of the lone fight of these three against big-time graft in the heart of the world's mightiest empire. But read on.

The film opens with Marcellus making a passionate speech to the wavering S.P.Q.R., who have already delayed their decision about the wall for three years. He warns of the danger from the Carthaginians, and ends with a great peroration. This is above politics, he says. '*Hoc est aliquid magnum, majus omnibus nobis. Per totam orbem, sunt milia milia populorum; parvi populi, solum similes nobis, cum hoc spe in cordibus suis.*' ('This is something big, bigger than all of us. All over the world there are millions of people; little people just like you and me, with this hope in their hearts. . . .')

The S.P.Q.R. applaud warmly. The contract is given to Balbus, and it is while they are crowding round to congratulate him that he first sees Julia. It is love at first sight. '*Nonne* aliquis tibi dixit te pulchram esse?*' ('Did anyone ever tell you you're beautiful?') he asks. He dates her for the evening. '*Ego te feram ad parvum locum quem cognosco, solum nos duo.*' ('I'll take you to a little place I know, just the two of us.') '*Ubi fuistis omnem vitam meam?*' asks Julia. ('Where have you been all my life?')

But this idyll is shattered by the machinations of a grafter called Caesar Romerus, of whom he has already been warned by Julia, '*Iste homo est periculosus*' ('That man is dangerous'). Romerus puts the word about that Marcellus, who is a stone merchant, is supplying Balbus with faked stones, made of plaster, for the wall. Balbus, angered by the rumours, goes down to inspect the wall, and finds to his horror that they *are* faked stones.

That night, dining with Julia, he is moody. '*Num† est altera mulier?*' ('Is there another woman?') she asks. He confesses his doubts about her father's honesty, and there is a quarrel in which he accuses her of making love to him to shield Marcellus. '*Nolo talem amorem.*' ('I don't want that kind of love.') '*O mel, da mihi fracturam, et tibi demonstrabo quod non est vere.*'

---

* Question expecting the answer 'Yes'.
† Question expecting the answer 'No'.

('Gee, honey, give me a break, and I'll prove it isn't true.')
'Mel, debes audire,' she implores. ('Honey, you've got to
listen.')

But Balbus is unmoved. He rises stiffly. *'Hoc est vale'* ('This
is good-bye'), he grates. Broken-hearted, Julia walks home
alone. She hears voices coming from a cellar, and listens. It
is Romerus and his associates, who are in league with the
Carthaginians, plotting to substitute more fake stones.
Startled, she cries, *'Sic illud est ludus tuus.'* ('So that's your
game.')

Romerus hears the intruder, and she is caught. *'Tu mane
ex hoc, soror'* ('You stay out of this, sister'), he snarls as she
is kidnapped. Next day, in a Rome worried by the news that
the enemy is throwing forces across the river, a repentant
Balbus is frantic at Julia's disappearance....

It would spoil the suspense of this mighty drama to reveal
how Balbus, on bail awaiting a corruption charge with Marcellus tracks down Romerus and rescues Julia. *'Cape illud'*
('Take that'), he grits, as his fist rams home on the grafter's
chin; and how the pair, dishevelled but reunited, arrive at
a dramatic moment in the trial of Marcellus. But look out
for the posters:

*Nunc, BALBI MURUS, maximum spectaculum omnis tem-
poris.* (Now, THE WALL OF BALBUS, the greatest spectacle of all time....)

ADVICE TO HUSBANDS

Spring-cleaning is a basic human experience. Faced in the right way, it sets the seal on married love. In these days, however, for many young couples it holds needless terrors. The strains and stresses of modern civilization cause husbands to regard this beautiful, *natural* function with fear, sometimes with real horror. Instead of seeking advice from experts they fill their minds with half-digested stories of difficult cases. Older husbands, who ought to know better, seem to get a perverse pleasure from recounting ghoulish legends, most of them mere old husbands' tales. Many perfectly healthy young men have been frightened into a 'difficult' experience by hearing of 'Mr W., whose first one took five weeks'. Such stories do nothing but harm, and serve only to shatter that calm relaxation which is essential to a successful deliv ... to a successful Spring-cleaning.

I shall attempt in this article to answer a few of the questions most commonly put to me about Spring-cleaning. But before this, it is essential for husbands to have the right attitude in general. Discuss it with your wife, and try to see that Spring-cleaning is not simply the result of a blind pleasure-urge on her part. Above all, do not resent it. You are partners in a great enterprise that has gone on since the beginning of time. Without Spring-cleaning, the race would die out. In the days of cave-women, it was only when the year's collection of stones and bones was moved out that there was room for more food, for more life, more progress. Today, in this great act of bringing a brand-new home into the world, you are carrying on the torch for posterity, ensuring that your country is not buried under piles of old newspapers, choked with dust, or dead from boredom through looking at furniture in the same position for two or even three years. You should have a real love and sense of wonder for this vast potential power in your wife, who fertilizes you and your home, and enables you to shed a skin, like a snake. Even if you have a hard time (and even today it is no good denying that modern knowledge is sometimes powerless to avoid complications, such as heavy paint bills, or long uncomfortable periods when all the chairs are upside-down in between the main upheavals) try to relax; think of that magic moment when, for the first time, you will see your wonderful new home.

A word to wives. Be forbearing with your husband at this time. If he has strange cravings, for unusual drinks perhaps; or if he flies into unreasonable passions, humour him. Remember that this is nature's way of showing that his time is near; he is about to produce wonderful new paints, new distempers, and samples for curtains and carpets from his pocket. So give him the stability and rest that he so deeply needs from you now.

In a long experience of such cases I have found that those on the threshold of an 'event' usually have more or less the same queries. Here are some of the main ones.

Should I have my Spring-cleaning at home or in hospital?

This is always a difficult question to answer. Ideally speaking, the unique bond between husband and wife at this time demands that you should have it naturally in your own home. Unfortunately, however, modern civilized man is not like the sturdy people of peasant countries, where the bread-winner often carries on in the fields within a matter of hours after his hovel has been swept out. Modern mental hospitals, with every resource at their disposal for dealing with badly frayed nerves in emergency cases, are a facility one cannot afford to overlook. And today there is also a growing tendency for men to have their Spring-cleaning in residential clubs or hotels. Generally speaking, this decision is largely determined by economics; if you live in a small house you will probably find it more convenient to stay there.

Is it dangerous to have one every year?

No. Provided proper care is taken there is no reason why a healthy man should not go on having Spring-cleaning right up to his seventieth year.

We have been married for seven years but have not had a Spring-cleaning yet. The doctor says I am quite normal. What should I do?

First satisfy yourself, honestly, that you have no hidden fears or reservations. Then you should have a frank talk with a reputable firm of interior decorators. But there is no way of telling whether the fault lies with your wife until *after a successful Spring-cleaning by them*, and this is why it is vitally necessary to be honest with yourself first. Artificial methods of this kind, unless used with the help of contractors who have been personally recommended to you, can be fraught with danger. Many men who have mistakenly used them, thinking unjustifiably that the fault lay with their wives, have suffered for years after the event from after-effects such as 'Inverted Pocket', 'Bill Shock', and 'Wasp's Disease' (in which the victim cries out incessantly that he has been stung).

What diet do you recommend?

As a general rule I always advise, as part of the layette, a large number of tins ... in the average household, about forty. But I have known many successful cases, of average duration (seven to ten days) where the patient has managed entirely on sandwiches. These, however, are rather rich in carbohydrates, and in any case the effort of opening tins is quite enough for the average patient, who should conserve as much energy as possible for the task in hand. The tins should, however, be varied by one or two very large meals, at which the wife may or may not be present, in a hotel. The main thing to remember is plenty to drink.

Ought I to help by moving smaller articles of furniture, filling buckets, etc.?

On no account. Nature has fore-ordained an active role for women, a passive one for men. Women are physically equipped to find food and nourishment for their partners while they are going through this phase. Your job is to produce, after the quiet of a calm gestation, the spiritual and financial resources for the grand mutual task of transformation of the house. This is quite enough. Leave the physical side of it to the woman, and relax. During your Spring-cleaning many delicate psychological factors come into play; and it is possible that you may feel a groundless 'guilt' at the loving trouble which is being expended on you. You should ignore it; and a wise wife will help to laugh these fears away.

OUTSIDE, LOOKING IN

It is extraordinary how the everyday pursuit of money, in which we are all engaged, has somehow come to be regarded as purely practical, a cold, calculating business that has nothing to do with dreams. Dreams are thought, in our civilization, to belong strictly to off-duty hours, whether we sink passively into the limbo of Hollywood shades or purposefully set off to a concert hall, where our face becomes one of a row, all expectant, all expecting too much, all expecting the great cries of the orchestra to blind us, to dissolve us, to bring us to It.

Yet the fact is that nearly all of us have one or two dreams about money. One dream is that when we are rich we shall live more gaudy, more exotic, happier lives, even – although one look at the miserable thin people in the long black saloons that whistle past us ought to disprove *that*. The other (and this is my dream) conceives of life as a series of concentric platforms, all revolving in the same direction, but at varying speeds, the fastest on the outside. To be poor is to be on the outside circle, where all the goods you acquire are flung off by sheer centrifugal force. You have a job to stay on the platform yourself, let alone hold on to a lot of parcels.

You find, for instance, that you have got to have a new pair of shoes, so you rush into a shop and buy some; some cheap ones, and they are worn out in three months. But if you were on one of the inner platforms you would go calmly into a rather splendid shop and buy the sort of shoes that are bought by men on leave in London from Africa, or down from their Scottish moorland estates. Twenty years later these men are still wearing the same shoes, they photograph them with mud on, they write letters which may be inspected at the head office of the shoe firm.

But the point is that after these twenty years inner-circle men have spent far less on shoes than outside men. And right in the centre of the dream there are calm, Blakean figures sitting motionless, for the centre platform does not move at all. At the centre, their possessions are so good that they never need to buy anything else, or if a replacement ever is necessary the thing replaced is still in such good condition that the overall outlay is small.

This dream is further complicated by the illogicality found in all dreams, for *one lives on several platforms at once.* Thus, I buy what I think is a good car (well, a better car than its predecessor, which was made in 1928) and I leave it for a moment on one of the inner platforms while I go to another part of the same platform to get some good clothes. I buy a tremendously good jacket of Harris tweed, dyed with vegetable dyes by peasants, having strong whitish threads like lion's whiskers in it; a coat a third of an inch thick, a coat I will still be wearing as a gentle old man in thirty years' time, when it will be faded, but still clearly *good.*

I struggle back with this coat to the place where I left the car – and it has gone, it has slid off to an outer platform where it really belongs. I was deceived, it wants a new back axle, a respray.... I feel like that Dutch boy who put his finger in the hole in the dyke, then his hand, then his arm, then his shoulder ... help! help, in the windy night.

We people on the outer platforms, we live in the world of Heraclitus, where everything is flux. Things change before our very eyes, there is no time to contemplate the inner essence of objects. At the moment, my wireless is changing. When I bought it, not all that long ago, from a man I used to meet occasionally at lunch, it seemed to me a wonderfully good and sophisticated wireless. It was a portable radiogram as well. It looked like a suitcase, and when you opened the lid, inside which the aerial was cunningly laced, there were the turntable and the dials. But now I see I was on a very outer platform when I bought it.

Its portability is a myth; it weighs just as much as an ordinary radiogram (and who wants to move a radiogram anyway? There's only one room in any house where a radiogram belongs). The catch that holds the silly lid up isn't reliable, and sometimes it has fallen down when a record was playing. It doesn't seem to be properly insulated, and when I touch it I get a vibrating sensation, an embryonic electric shock.

I always thought there was something definite about electrical machinery – either it works or it doesn't – until the motor in this thing simply got *tired*, as though overcome by the weight of the pick-up (admittedly much heavier than those featherweight crystal things they have on the inner circle). It made a brisk Haydn symphony sound like a lugubrious procession of zombies in a vault. So I took the motor out. It left a diamond-shaped hole in the casing. Our cat had three kittens at the time, and one of them got through this hole to play with the wiring. I lugged the whole contraption to the shop. It got less portable at every step, and banged against my knees. I told the man it had had a kitten inside. He did his best, but it has never been the same since. There is a cat influence in it, a hint of witches and devils. It howls and crackles, it gets supernatural hate stations that simply put out a diabolical throaty growling. . . .

That's what it is about the inner platform. They don't have cats in their wirelesses.

THE ANNUAL LAMP COMPANY

Life in a modern city, full of chance sights and associations blown away into infinity before their implications can be grasped, is like music, which can never be halted and fully examined at any particular point. We walk down the street, and a van passes bearing the extraordinary legend 'C. S. Rolls and Co, Guillotine Knife Grinders, 2–4 Bleeding Heart Yard.' Before we have time to imagine this appalling shambles we see a shop full of garden furniture; we wonder who on earth has so much money that he can spare £80 for a chintz-covered settee suspended in a kind of derrick.

Eighty pounds! It would take five men half an hour to erect this thing, pinching their thumbs and cursing, and by that time, in England, it would be raining, and – but here comes a fire engine.

There is a further musical parallel for this multiplicity. In the basic community of Plato's *Republic* there are at first only the husbandmen, the builders, the tailors, and the shoe-makers; merchants come later. So, too, there were in the beginning the Greek modes, and later, in the eighteenth century, the diatonic scale, precise and limited. But now there is atonalism, where everything merges into everything else – just as, walking through London, we are aware of infinite gradations of commercial activity going on in little offices and workshops, up flights of uncarpeted wooden stairs, where typewriters tap behind closed doors: a network of voices, bells, and voices, murmuring or harsh, all indirectly having to do with us, changing our lives – a shadow-real activity endlessly filling the air above our heads, on second and third floors.

Let us attempt the impossible for a minute, let us stop the record of this vast music; let us examine two of these activities. Let us consider the writing I saw last week on two windows facing each other in a street near Tottenham Court Road; *Annual Lamp Company*, and *Glass Benders*.

These seem to represent a complexity beyond which civilization can advance no further. What extraordinary, unguessed-at need do they satisfy? Annual lamps. At first sight the mind boggles, there seems no connexion whatever between these amazingly disparate words. We might as well have seen, on these windows, 'Pantomime Crankshaft Company', 'Mousetrap Wind Bros.', 'Egg Navigation Consultants', or 'Straw Pianos, Ltd'. Do they make a tremendously ornate lamp, like the hat of Edward Lear's Quangle Wangle

> *...with ribbons and bibbons on every side*
> *And bells, and buttons, and loops, and lace*

– a lamp so complicated that it takes a year to make? Is it, perhaps, a huge lighthouse lamp, with parabolic reflectors, big enough to have a bathroom inside, like that organ at Atlantic City?

But the very size of the modest premises belies these monstrous conjectures. Come, let us be more practical, more prosaic. It exists, this annual lamp. People gain their livelihoods by it. Perhaps there is an ordinary lamp factory, but it changes its directors every year, electing them from among the workers – a cross between the Co-op and the John Lewis partnership. Perhaps it is a kiddies' novelty lamp, to enable them to read their Christmas annuals under the bedclothes. Perhaps it is fairy lights for Christmas trees, or simply a lamp guaranteed to last one year....

But no, all these pictures dissolve as soon as we examine them closely. So, too, do our notions of the glass benders, holding their breath as a tiny increase of pressure is applied, then relaxing as they hear the familiar sharp cracking sound, sweeping the fragments of glass off the floor and putting them in a vat, to start all over again.

Wait a minute, though. Could there possibly be any connexion between the two? Could it be that, one November afternoon, as the needle on the gauge mounts higher and higher, the glass does *not* crack? Significant glances are exchanged, like those of the masked surgeons in screen operations, until finally the glass is bent right round, in a perfect cylinder.

Yes, see them proudly carrying it across the road to the Annual Lamp Co. 'H'm, thought you'd never make it this year,' grunts the Lampmaster, 'still, it's a beautiful job. Now we can get on with our lamp. Well, see you next year. Let's have your invoice, won't you?' And the deputation goes back, walking through the silent-roaring traffic, back up the wooden stairs into the formless tide of music, into the undreamable dream of the infinite city.

SPRING SONG

Of the Spring would I sing, now that every living thing
Is a rocket-burst, a sun-flash of Creation;
These metaphors, I hope, will conceal that I'm a dope
When it comes to name and local habitation.

  Oh, that bush of whatsaname is a mass of golden flame
  And the snowy almond makes my heart feel merry –
  No, wait a bit – I think that the almond is the pink,
  This one is labelled *Prunus* (is that cherry?)
  Hark! The Pentecostal breeze is a voice among the trees
  (Now, is the bark striated, are leaves dentifoliated?)
  I am just an urban bloke, who can recognize an oak
  But ask me 'birch or larch?' and you fill me with unease.
  For beauty I'm rapacious, I adore the bed herbaceous,
  Especially this reddish-purple dahlia;
  But the things I thought I *knew* all turn out to be untrue –
  It's a *geum*. I'm a botanistic failure.
  Each merry month of May as I find I'm no Linnaeus
  I wander in a wonderland of Latin,
  In the mystic parks where I go there are banks of impetigo
  And fields of erysipelas I've sat in.
  As sticky buds get buddleia my nature lore gets muddlier,
  And no amount of garden-book reading
  Will cure me of nemesia or make it any easier
  To say at once 'Look! Love-lies-bleeding!'
  There's a multitude of words for the flashing flocks of
    birds
  My neighbour's knowledge widens where mine narrows,

All I can point out with no shadow of a doubt
Are the *passeres domestici*, or sparrows;
But my neighbour says with glee 'There's a *nuthatch* in
  my tree!'
He seems to know it all by intuition,
I look at coloured plates full of speckled chests and pates
But vain is my perusal of wheatear and ring-ousel,
The birds I see escape my definition.
When I try to guess their song I am nearly always wrong
Although in Goldsmith's *Animated Nature*
I have read that words like this in the nightingale mean
  bliss:

> *Quio, didl li lulyie*
> *Hagurr, gurr quipio*
> *Hezezezezezezezeze couior ho dze hoi*
> *Kigaigaigaigaigaigaigaigai couior dziodzio pi*

– But a short, explosive *Fitt!* just means 'I hate yer!'
I am clueless but poetic. I am not apologetic,
  A flower quite transcends the name it bears
  And in Spring, let experts note, though they have the world
    by rote,
My stimulus from primulas is similar to theirs.

MISKIN

Rivers and urban life take each other mutually by surprise. To float down a river is to see an unsuspected back view of civilization – the blank sides of breweries, curious parks, inaccessible pubs, the evening rose-gardens of Edwardian houses, closed-looking green sheds belonging to improbable clubs. And to come upon a river in a town is somehow to doubt the comfortable lamp-posts and Odeons; to be reminded by this quiet arm of primordial water, this tame piece of infinity, that life is not purely a municipal affair, but is interlaced with tributaries from the vast, unpredictable sea of chance. The most jaded motorist, glimpsing the black water through the balustrade of the urban bridge, has some faint echo of the feeling that

In the breaking of bridges
Is treason and doom.

Moreover, all rivers have a quintessential rightness. The Severn, even at its most anglicized, say at Worcester, retains a Celtic flavour; a *frisson* of little grey waves confronts the smooth English cathedral with a reminder of plaintive song in vague Welsh hills. The Clyde looks forward to sharp riveters in the morning air, and backward to clear brown pools. And, most archetypal of all, the Thames carries a whisper of otherness through England, from this mysterious Lechlade, which is halfway to Wales, to London, where the Houses of Parliament look out as on a grey sea.

Mysteries dwell on the banks of the Thames. Once, drifting idly along near Walton, I opened my eyes to see a brick wall gliding past, bearing the legend:

GRIDLEY MISKIN. DOOR STORE

Only a week later I observed at Chiswick a signboard which indubitably said:

SUBMERGED LOG COMPANY

There is a fundamental rightness about these. Here, we think, are just the quiet but rather mysterious occupations we would expect to find followed on the banks of a river. Borne on the gentle stream of conjecture, we remember that there is a mystery of doors, as there is of bridges. From the first we imagine this store to be more than merely the adjunct of a timber business. It has more than commercial implications. Perhaps here, by the sliding river, is a kind of reference library of doors. To this dim, silent warehouse, smelling of sawdust, come unimaginable door enthusiasts, to gaze at vast cathedral doors, to take out on loan eighteenth-century doors painted with nymphs and shepherds, to gaze entranced at a collection of tiny doll's-house doors, or intricate doors designed for those experiments with mice and concealed food.

But, as we ponder, even this does not seem to match the matchless name of Gridley Miskin. For it seems as though the 'Gridley' stands for the human, commercial side of things (you could have a bank, or a club, called Gridley's), whereas 'Miskin' is for the damp, elusive water spirit, for the sound of the breeze in riverside willows, sighing *miskin miskin* on summer afternoons.

Nor does ordinary conjecture provide a satisfactory picture of the Submerged Log Company. We cannot really imagine a firm for selling sodden tree trunks, or for providing divers to rescue nautical records carelessly thrown overboard. We reject, too, the conceit that an *ordinary* Log Company was long ago swallowed up, like Atlantis, in some extraordinary flood, so that the top of an antique sawmill comes above the surface at low waters and the villagers of Chiswick tell of ghostly sawing noises at night.

No, it is by the shivered images of river reflection that we perceive the obscure, sub-aqueous connexion between these two. Down in a watery green light, we know not where, these submerged logs are worked upon with soundless tools. They are fashioned into doors – the Doors of Miskin. These doors are *upside-down*. They are there and not there. They open into dreamy, upside-down fields, where vague figures and cloudy cities swim in a refracted light; where far-off, deep-down music, *miskin* music, wraps everything in a drowned harmony.

Down here is no clear-cut polity, with a Submerged Stock Exchange and a Submerged Post Office. Down here, forms merge into one another. *Miskin* is a concept allied to the Hindu *atman*, which is at once the individual soul and the world. *Miskin* has to do with the watery origin of creation, when no men troubled the bright flood. *Miskin* is the spirit of all rivers. The concrete facts of Reading or Maidenhead, with their pillar-boxes and early-closing days, are subtly permeated by this vague *miskin*; the infinite water of possibility from which all actual things emerge.

SCOTCH MISTERY

Taghairm, *ta'garm. n.* In the Scottish Highlands, divination; esp. inspiration sought by lying in a bullock's hide behind a waterfall. (Gael.) – *Chambers's Twentieth Century Dictionary*

The train moved slowly across the high, rain-washed moor, a tiny human activity under the enormous silent tumult of an Atlantic sunset. Watery purple and gold light streamed levelly into the dusty compartment of which Hugo Thisbee was the only occupant. All day he had travelled northwards through an ennui of grey rain, and now the day had flowered into this huge glory, this apotheosis, this revelation; a climax arbitrary, unexpected, *given.*

Hugo felt disturbed. All this skiey splendour, at once a spectacle and somehow a statement, seemed to require from him a response, an activity. But, even as he projected into the riding clouds his images of crying human history, of half-heard music, of kings and ghosts and lovers, he was aware of a lack, a loneliness, a separation. The world is there, it beckons to us, but the moment we speak we must stop listening to it. We must do something to be inspired, to get to the eternal fountain, but we don't know what it is we must do. If only inspiration and meaning were a planned activity –

'Auchterhellweet! Auchterhellweet!' The cry echoing along the little station interrupted Hugo's reverie. Clear brown water tumbled among rocks beside the line. Above its purling there was the sound of a deeper, distant booming; and looking up into a darkening cleft Hugo could just make out, in the cold after-sunset-light, a hundred-foot shaft of falling water.

This seemed a likely place. Hugo got out. The train puffed

49

away, and soon there was only the sound of water to be heard. The colours faded from things. The station-master of Auchterhellweet, who was also the porter, signalman, and ticket collector, paused from lighting the oil lamps to take Hugo's ticket.

'I – er – know this sounds a bit silly,' said Hugo, 'but do you possibly know where I could get a bullock's hide. I – well, I thought this looked like grazing country as we came along, and I –'

'Losh, you're anither o' yon dafties. Weel, I dinna ken whit ye're a' daein' the noo. But Willy McGregor'll likely be havin' one in his wee shop. He'll no be fashed at ye roustlin' him oot if ye tell him I sent ye.'

Ten minutes later, Hugo was climbing painfully up the defile, dragging the great skin behind him. It seemed to get heavier at every step. It was nearly dark when he came to a high rocky ledge that seemed to go right behind the thundering torrent, and there he sat down to rest. Suddenly, an extraordinary figure detached itself from the shadows – something like Bottom, having legs of a man and the head not of an ass, but of a bull.

'Good heavens! Hugo Thisbee!' said a voice, instantly recognizable as that of Randall Harkness, a writer on aesthetics whom he had met occasionally in King's Road pubs. 'My dear, what *have* you got there? I say, a *real* bullock. How jolly enterprising! I only hired mine from Gardners. But it has got a head and yours hasn't. Rather chic, don't you think? Look, this is my bullock dance.' He pranced about. 'I've just popped out for a smoke – the matches won't strike in there. I've been lying there all day in this damn thing. I feel just as dreary as ever, no ideas at all. I say, I *am* pleased to see you, the others are terrible bores.'

'The others?' said Hugo.

'Why yes. There aren't many waterfalls you can lie behind in Scotland, and this is the only one near a railway station. You come up here for a spot of the old *taghairm*, you'll generally find some of the boys and girls. Somebody must have spread the word at a P.E.N. conference.'

'How many are there?'

'Oh, about a dozen. It's got rather like The Method, nowa-days. In fact, there is one American here. Rather a nice man, called Budd Lee – or is it Lee Budd? He was at a Fiction Workshop. I expect they *chisel* their prose, hna hna hna! – only he's got a waterproof typewriter. But there's a lot of bio-graphers this year. I don't think they *count*, do you? They're trying to wangle some grant or other to build a kind of shed thing on the ledge to keep the water out. I'm sure it won't work then.'

Harkness threw down his cigarette and stretched. 'Still, I got cracking reviews for *Many a Dark Star*, and I got the idea for it up here in '54 when there was only me, a crazy old shepherd, and a sweet old palmist thing called Madame La Rosa; she always comes for the divination. Ah well, back to the old trance-like ecstasy. I've had Victor's advance, you know, and I haven't written a word yet. It just won't *come*. Come on in and meet Madame La – here I say, *Hugo!*'

But Hugo had disappeared and was climbing on, up the dark mountain, alone.

BELIEVING IN WEAVING

I muse among the magic of museums
From ritzy (the Uffizi) to that goodly other
   Harrods (V and A)
And marvel at the manifold *Te Deums*
In sacramental stone and paint and clay,
The Unseen Form in many forms made plastic;
From knotty Buonarotti to the dotty men
   who do it all with blots
All artists find me quite enthusiastic,
From Praxiteles and Phidias to the shock-the-
   bourgeois hideous,
From Henry Moore to neolithic pots,
The Lippo Lippi triptych, the simple and
   the cryptic I admire,
At any hint of tedium I find another medium –
A statue not in stone, but bits of wire;
What a solace is the Wallace, all majolica and monster
   French clocks,
But one blind spot I seem to have in galleries
(Where Madonnas smile upon us, where the Beautiful and
   True is piled in stocks) –
I simply can't waste energy, or calories
On *tapestries*. It's sophistry not owning that I find them
   stumbling-blocks.

      Tapestries are all a bore
      Enormous scenes of love or war,
      Men with spears on rearing horses

(Much too *fat* for our racecourses)
Boars and tusks and guns and blood,
Victims trampled in the mud,
Or, in scenes of peace and plenty
Measuring fifty feet by twenty
Enormous picnics in a glade
Where Cupid does a roaring trade
Great big nymphs and great big shepherds,
Great big men in skins of leopards,
All one colour, due to age –
A rather horrid kind of beige.
Tapestries must seize their chances
Of receiving casual glances
In the corridors between
Rooms with things that *must* be seen
As I haste towards Botticellis
Wondering what that musty smell is.

Artist-weavers, don't despair
(Lurçat, do not tear your hair!)
Many folk must find bewitching
All this anecdotal stitching
Or curators couldn't face
Giving it such *miles* of space.

PARTY PIECE

One of the most obvious proofs that Things are against Men is provided by the piano. For this instrument will hardly ever suffer itself to be played by those whose idea of earthly happiness would be the ability to go to a shining dark Blüthner in a room full of flowers and release a thundering torrent of Brahms or Chopin. The only people who actually *can* do this sort of thing always look as if they were bored to death by it.

One has only to look at the inscrutable faces of dance-band pianists, or at accompanists, as they sit, anonymous, in the shadows beyond the limelight, on the left-hand side of the stage, while the nonchalant, contemptuous skill of their arpeggios redeems the amateurishness of the girl in blue tulle at the microphone. Sometimes they look so sardonic and world-weary that one even wonders if they didn't begin like the Blüthner-and-flowers people, like us, and then sell their souls to the Devil; for the explanation that they just *look* detached, to deceive the piano, doesn't hold water. When *I* remember not to bite my tongue and try to look nonchalant I just hit more wrong notes than ever.

And it isn't that I don't, or didn't, practise, either. For a long time after the war I practised two hours a day, paying 1s. 6d. an hour for one of a honeycomb of studios with brown linoleum floors and feeble gas-fires and steel engravings of the great composers. The building vibrated at all hours of the day with music made by all kinds of people: sad men of fifty, with bowler hats, pegging away at simple Mozart sonatas; virtuosi playing the Brahms–Handel variations;

tenors, who one somehow felt all had the Christian name Arthur, squawking 'naming-the-enemy-naming-the-enemy-naming-the-enemy' all down the scale.

But I never achieved any spontaneity. It is true that I learned to play a few pieces, but they were all of the mathematical, geometrical kind that anyone with intelligence and perseverance can learn synthetically. They were not the kind of music to play at parties.

Yet the awful thing is that, by some fatal process which I cannot analyse and never seem to be able to stop, I always *do* find myself playing them at parties. My host catches me, perhaps in a moment when I am looking at the piano. 'Let's have some music,' he says; 'you play the piano, don't you?' Somehow I can't look churlish and deny all knowledge of it, and I hear myself saying, in the sudden silence which has now descended on the room: 'I can't play party music; I only know a few Bach pieces.'

'Oh, I love Bach,' says a woman. I can see they all think I have one of those tremendous Tausig arrangements of the organ works up my sleeve. I cannot explain that my pieces are, in fact, the Two-Part Invention in F Major, a Prelude in A Flat from the 48, and, surprisingly, the Prelude of the famous D Minor organ toccata (for I once learned the organ, which I found less romantic and more mathematical, and therefore easier, than the piano).

So I play the D Minor. Diddle OM, diddle iddle ER der. The opening, so magisterial in an echoing church, sounds absurdly exhibitionist. Too late I realize that this sort of thing succeeds only if played by brilliant pianists at the kind of party one sees on the films, where the men have imperial beards and monocles and the women have fans and everybody has just come back from the Opera. A sardonic-looking man, of whom I have been uneasily aware all the evening, starts a whispered conversation with a girl for whom he is pouring a drink. Another girl comes in, and there is a long fuss about finding her a seat.

I finish the Prelude. There is mild applause. The woman who said she liked Bach is sitting at the end of the piano, and I find myself involved in a long, intense conversation with her. The party flows gaily on round us, with pompous words like *Zeitgeist* occasionally bouncing from our corner into the general earshot.

Presently the sardonic man sits at the piano and begins an absolutely hopeless performance of popular tunes. He plays the melody in octaves and the same chord all the time with his left hand, giving the familiar tunes a curious modal, Hebridean folk-song feeling. It is terrible. But to my astonishment everybody sings, knowing the words, asking him for more. 'Can you play "Stormy Weather"?' they say. He can certainly play the left hand, because it'll be exactly the same, I think nastily.

More than ever I wish I could rattle off syncopated music like those accompanists. But I expect if I went back to the studios and slaved at that for two years, like the man in the advertisement who used to say 'My friends were amazed', by the time I had achieved anything there would be a great vogue for Bach at parties.

THEATRE OPERATION

When I found that the amateur dramatic society which I had joined always gave one performance at a hospital, it was too late to withdraw. I ought to have withdrawn earlier, anyhow; the friend who ran it had told me they were going to do *You Can't Take It With You*, and I had hoped to be cast as the delightful lunatic who makes fireworks in the basement and ends Act One with an enormous explosion. I hadn't bargained for playing Captain Wickham, in *Pride and Prejudice*, to a helpless audience of convalescents.

The hospital was in North London, in what had once been a country estate where landaulettes rolled up to a lawn dotted with parasols; but now, as we arrived with the fruits of our winter rehearsal, it was just a sad urban wood surrounded by villas. The place was deathly silent. The company, carrying suitcases, assembled in the Gothic porch, under a Victorian coat-of-arms, and instinctively stopped chattering when the producer pulled a great wrought-iron handle, and a distant bell was heard.

I was suddenly filled with panic. Although we had been assured that 'our friends at the hospital' were looking forward to our visit, it seemed to me now an appalling presumption that we should attempt to create the warm magic of the theatre in this naked, functional place. Wildly I tried to recall what I had been told about Noël Coward, alone on a bare platform in the Middle East, gradually getting five thousand restive troops to eat out of his hand ... after all, we should at least have bed screens for curtains.

The men changed in a room full of white, glass-fronted

cabinets containing little bottles. There was the awful coconut smell of make-up. We were all given a little duplicated slip which said '*There is no back cloth*. If you come off R and have to reappear L, go up hall steps, along passage, through little door on right, down iron staircase, through door, through recreation room, up stairs, Vice versa for L to R.'

I should have liked very much to practise this route before going on, since it looked as deceptively detailed as the instructions, shouted from other people's sitting-rooms when you are in their kitchen, about how to find the sugar. They always have to come themselves in the end, just as I should have liked the writer of these directions to demonstrate his route. But there was no time. Our Mozart divertimento stole out across the darkened Victorian drawing-room. The gracious, complicated sentences began. '*It is a reflection on every gentleman present that one so fair should lack an escort ...*' and suddenly I was offstage, R.

My splendid officer's uniform had no pockets, so I had lost the directions. There was nobody to ask. I went up the hall steps. Along passage. Little door – no, not that one. Another door – good, here's the iron staircase. An outside fire-escape. It was raining. I got half-way down, then I met Lady Catherine de Burgh, in a billowing yellow dress, coming up. My sword stuck in the railings. I got out of the belt and backed up the stairs to let her pass. As she brushed by the sword belt she freed it. It fell with a clatter on to some dustbins below. A nurse opened a window, and betrayed no surprise when a British officer of the Napoleonic War period on the fire-escape asked her for a box of matches. I went right down to the bottom, and began striking matches to find my sword among the dustbins, in the pouring rain.

I opened a door, but it revealed the boiler-room. I asked an astonished man with a shovel where the recreation room was. 'Next floor,' he said. I felt glad it wasn't a mental hospital. On the next floor there were two doors, one locked. The unlocked one opened into a long kitchen, full of maids at aluminium-topped tables. I strode down this room, with my sword; there was no time for dallying, my big scene with

Lydia must be nearly due, and there was a big, important sort of door at the other end which looked as if it led into some more public domain. I was half-way down before I saw it was only a cupboard.

I strode back again, and up the iron staircase. I arrived, breathless and wet, on the same side of the stage that I had come off, just in time for my scene with Lydia, who was looking expectantly for me in the other direction. I am sure the patients, or rather the audience, thought I was going to pant out the news of Waterloo rather than make love.

I discovered two more doors into that kitchen; in fact I went through it four times. They must have thought I was a stage army. After the play I got the first glimpse I have ever had behind medical inscrutability. We were invited to refreshments in the recreation room. When I saw the liberal bar and the enormous array of excellent food, I quite saw why it had been locked.

EUSTON SLEEPERS

It is curiously difficult to feel self-assured when ringing up a railway. To begin with, there is the feeling that one is not so clever as one's friends, who have Bradshaws on their well-kept bookshelves, through which they could flip confidently and find the right answer even if they wanted to go, on a Sunday, to Parkgate and Rawmarsh (Yorks), calling at Yarmouth on the way; whereas one cannot, oneself, even read the main-line time-tables posted up at stations. On these bleak white sheets, as uncompromising as the Finance Act, there are always three dots, instead of a time, at the place one wants to go to; and some trains appear to leave places before they arrive there.

There is, however, an even more uneasy feeling – a feeling that in telephoning one has become an Unauthorized Person backstage of the railway. 'Oh, you want Passenger Inquiries,' says a distant female voice in a tone which suggests that one has interrupted its owner from moving model trains with a rake over a huge table-map. Of course I want Passenger Inquiries. One of these days I shall bark into the phone, before they have time to say anything, 'Now see here, about these demurrage charges on bulk tariff consignments. . . .'

There follows a long, hollow silence, punctuated by somebody making squeaky noises with a toy balloon, or by frantic clickings, like desperate machine-gun fire, as the call is transferred from the slick, sophisticated Post Office system to the heavy, ironclad telephones and tremendous alarm bells of the railway; it is easy to visualize the wires looped along black walls, through tunnels and warehouses, and indeed it would not be surprising if the call were finally answered from one of those mysterious little sheds, just outside any big station, where men in shirtsleeves are always drinking tea by gaslight.

But I have never got so far backstage as I did last week, for I was answered immediately by a sepulchral, curiously dignified voice which simply said: 'Euston Sleepers!'

I couldn't have been more awed if it had said: 'Delphic Oracle, at your service' or 'Vestal Virgins, good morning.' So *that's* what they've got upstairs in that central hall at Euston, with its pillars and statues; the Seven Euston Sleepers, the tutelary deities of British Railways. How extraordinary that we should not have guessed; for we have all been faintly troubled by the feeling that in some way Euston is more than a station.

In an earlier article I suggested that it was a market, with regular auction sales of corrugated iron and hens and motorcycles and all the other things that one sees lying about there. But this was evidently only part of the truth. Fundamentally Euston is a temple, complete with Propylaeum (that arch thing is still called this) or Sacred Entrance. When we look at early prints of Euston, showing it in all its glory of cream stone against a Canaletto sky, it is easy to imagine the people coming through the Propylaeum with their gifts to the old railway gods. The houses that now huddle round Euston were a later development, as innkeepers and traders moved in to cater for the pilgrims.

It is right that railways should have deities, for they are a nation within a nation, with their curious lanes of private property stretching across our homely fields, their aloof stations brooding on the outskirts of our towns. The superficial observer might expect railway deities to be fierce spirits of flame, like Thor or Vulcan. But it is not so. The Seven Euston Sleepers, waited on by Porters and Porteresses of the Temple trimming lamps and performing other duties, stand for the stillness at the heart of action so well expressed by T. S. Eliot:

At the still point of the turning world, neither flesh nor fleshless;
Neither from nor towards; at the still point, there the dance is,

But neither arrest nor movement, and do not call it fixity,
Where past and future are gathered. Neither movement from nor
    towards,
Neither ascent nor decline. Except for the point, the still point,
There would be no dance, and there is only the dance.

The Seven Euston Sleepers (one for each of the six British
Railways districts and one for London) are the gods of the
quiet country stations, where no sound is heard but the wind
in the telephone wires and occasional signal bells; of the silent
cuttings through woods; of the motionless rows of carriages
at depots; of the pregnant silence when the train stops in a
tunnel. They are the silence at the heart of the solemn dance
of public transport.

DIESELIZATION

There is something at once startling and dreamy in the railway modernization scheme just announced. In one sense it is as revolutionary, in its resolve to do away with steam in Britain, as was Kemal Ataturk's abolition of the fez and the veil in Turkey. For let no one imagine that the change will affect the railways only.

Once those gaunt strong engines, named after people and places one has never quite heard of – Sir Henry Thomkins, Stindon Hall – are replaced by secretive diesels; once continuous brakes in goods trains have silenced for ever the night-long mysterious bing-bong-bang from misty, moonlit yards that for generations has told millions, in their warm beds, of our ancient, endless commerce; once the fretwork stations are replaced by pin-bright foyers, it is idle to suppose that the station hotels, the houses, and the blue brick churches and the people in them will remain the same. A certain openness, a certain ancestral earthy communion with fire and water and the lonely native hills, will have gone for ever.

It is even possible that in certain remote valleys steam will be kept defiantly alive; squads of reinforced railway police will meet sullen silence in their inquiries among villagers into reports of illegal steam trains seen, or heard, puffing at night under the dark Celtic mountains. Nay, the very climate may be changed. The British, instead of thinking primeval, empirical thoughts in a sort of permanent pre-Creation mist, an aboriginal foggy steam or steamy fog (one thinks of that marvellous, *basic* Turner picture *Rain, Steam and Speed*), may become just another Scandinavian country, matter-of-fact under a pale, clear sun. . . .

But in another sense there is about the whole thing a dream-like quality that does preserve a continuity with the old mystery of British steam, the ancient, abiding foundation of the modern world. Quite apart from the lordly, almost Oriental scope of the thing – the 4,600 new diesels, the element of magic in the way these vast moneys, twelve hundred million pounds, have suddenly been calmly produced so soon after all that fuss about financing the wage increase – we have these words of the Chairman of the Transport Commission himself:

Both the diesel and the electric locomotive lack the glamour which surrounds the mighty steam engine pounding through the night with the light of its fire glowing in the faces of the crew. There is something here of real importance, and we are honestly seeking a means to avoid losing all the romance which is attached to this great iron horse.

There speaks a true British voice. Sir Brian Robertson has commanded troops; he knows the strategic, practical arguments in favour of diesels. But clearly he also knows about this aspect, at once more fundamental and more true. It would be pleasant to think that what he envisages is the actual setting up of a Romance Department, with its headquarters, obviously, at Euston.

In this day and age the romance will have to be planned, artistic, formal. It cannot compete with the instinctive folk-jubilation in the first days of steam. When the Newcastle and Carlisle Railway was opened in 1838, thirteen special trains, containing 3,500 persons, crossed the fells.

Many flags and banners were carried [says Mr J. McLean's history] . . . the memory of 1815 stood out in words – 'The Glorious Eighteenth of June'; and *Vapor Vincit Omnia* proclaimed the might of steam. Alderman Thos. Wilson, a famous Tyneside poet, celebrated the occasion in verse. . . . The *Lightning*, with ten coaches, contained the Carlisle town band. Then *Tyne*, with its steam organ . . .

The whole vast peregrination took place in rain, fog, and

thunder; people fell in the river, trains ran into one another, Mayors got lost, ladies in silk dresses were marooned till after midnight in the misty hills that resounded to the loud statements of steam organs* and lusty bands.

After this Dionysiac age, the Romance Department must perforce seem Apollonian, self-conscious. It will employ poets (*The train on platform seven will take us all to heaven. Basingstoke beckons you. Yea, holy Salisbury, and on to the dark-wombed sea*); and actors, who, bearded or beautiful or exotic, will intensify the mystery we have always observed in people that are in *other* trains; and artists, who will hang marine stations with draperies of nets or paint murals of cog wheels for Birmingham (New Street).

But the Department will look backwards as well as forwards. Gently, authoritatively, it will shepherd steam from actuality into history. Over the centuries there will develop, at Euston, a sort of Tabernacle of Steam, where one holy, splendid, symbolic National Steam Train will be kept. On special occasions it will roll through the streets of London on special lines. It will go to Buckingham Palace for the Changing of the Guard; it will take conventions of foreign scholars to the British Museum and guests to the Royal Academy for the annual dinner; and it will lead the Lord Mayor's Show, that the plumes of steam may add their tradition to the ancient stones of London.

* And, incidentally, who ever heard of a diesel organ?

IN THE BEGINNING

(Now that my children are getting words right)

Lovely is language, and precious is precision,
Warmly I welcome you to wonderlands of words;
Expert grows your tongue – and yet I mourn another vision
Where meaning fluttered lightly as the carollings of birds:

> I shall miss, I must admit it,
> The early form of 'biscuit', *pittit*;
> Some precious thread for ever broke
> The day you ceased to ask for *mloke* –
> 'Milk', though clearer in intention,
> Lacks a certain fine invention.
> *Musegit* henceforth I'll not hear
> But with mere music soothe my ear
> (Called my *era* until lately).
> Now correctly and sedately
> *Dessidow* is 'dressing-gown'
> In which to *brekstett* we came down
> On Saturdays of relaxation
> (Not of *staxis* to the station);
> *Lunt*, the next meal, oft contained
> *Jarbies*, dully now explained
> As raspberries, consumed with ardour,
> Stored in *panatry*, or larder.
> Now your mind has made the jump
> To 'elephant' from *ellalump*
> I, too, must outgrow the habit
> And not *raddit* say but 'rabbit';
> I must learn to do without

The useful garden *weelybout*
(How pedantic seems, and narrow
The usual Common Noun 'wheelbarrow'!)
Humpty Dumpty must forget
Your name for him, *Egg-up-a-get*,
Miss Kitt's chonklit you'll not lick –
Just chocolate brought by Mr Crick;
Nor (last choice from samples multiple)
Will one again be ill in *hostipal*. . . .

Infancy, finish! And advance, articulation!
Leading you onwards to poetry and story –
But nothing you learn later, of lyric or oration,
Trails for your parents quite these clouds of glory.

BROTHERS IN BLOOM

Few examples of what is known in the advertising world as a direct mail campaign can be more successful than seed and bulb catalogues. They do, literally, germinate in the mind. They always arrive by the second post, which as wives know perhaps better than husbands is generally an anti-climax; there comes this rat-tat-tat; good, one thinks, a letter! All the ancient unconquerable hope springs up – it will contain miraculous good news, perhaps even some lovely money. One goes out into the sad afternoon hall and there, lying on the mat, is some boring circular or detergent coupon, dressed up to look like a silly bogus cheque.

But when it's a seed catalogue the mind is immediately led off into summer arbours, the lovely names intoxicate one: delphinium, larkspur, gladioli, and, look, Engelmann's Giant Pansy, we *must* have some giant pansies in the garden. We nearly always send for something; we fill up the order form in a dream.

Seed catalogues, like the whole business of gardening, make one feel simultaneously virtuous and voluptuary. One is assumed to be an artist, a poet, a lover of beauty; but one is also a responsible person, a householder, nay, a garden-holder.

The ambivalence of grave and gay is reflected in the catalogues themselves. Nine times out of ten the firm is So-and-so Brothers; and I have the feeling that one of these brothers is jolly, optimistic; he is the one who thinks up all the new names for roses, and writes all that lyrical stuff about 'star-like pure white flowers', 'glorious blood-red clusters', and so on. I think of him as Frank. But the other brother, Gideon, is a suspicious, gloomy character, who keeps the books, attends to the business side generally, and above all, writes the Terms of Business which are tucked away somewhere in every catalogue. Gideon can think of nothing but disaster. Some fool will spill paraffin on the seeds, or mix them up, so that carrots come instead of stocks, and then have the nerve to sue. 'Tarnation varmints 'll be the ruin of us,' mutters Gideon, and seizing a scratchy pen he scribbles *it is, therefore, not a condition of sale, neither do we warrant expressly or impliedly or under the terms of Sale of Goods Act 1893, that the seeds, bulbs, or roots shall correspond with the description under which they are sold, and we will not be responsible for the crop.*

Frank comes in with a marvellous tray of freesias. He is singing:

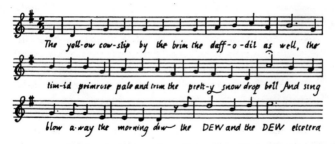

The yell-ow cow-slip by the brim the daff-o-dil as well, the tim-id primrose pale and trim the pret-ty snow drop bell And sing blow a-way the morning dew the DEW and the DEW etcetera

'Ah, Gid, 'tis good to be alive. Let's give people a bonus of these lovely freesias for all orders over 15s.'

'Why, thee gurt looby, happen we'll never deliver anythin' whiles there's sic a mort o' trouble in the world. Lookee, suppose one o' they gormed strikes hold up us delivery? Aye, thee'd not sing so blithe if I didn't put in thisyer. *Delivery to be made at the usual time unless prevented by war, blockade, revolution, prohibition of export or import, force majeure, failure of crop, or any other contingency beyond our control.*'

'Why, Gideon, old lad, hast forgotten earthquakes?' says Frank, flippantly; and nimbly dodging the secateurs hurled at him by Gideon he goes off, carolling among the rosebushes. Gideon, muttering, turns his attention from the foolishness of amateur gardeners to the villainous cunning of carriers. *In the case of goods damaged in transit, a clear signature should not be given, and the carriers should be notified in writing within three days that a claim will be made.* 'Heh, heh, that'll fox the varmints,' he cackles.

The thought of customers called, say, Robinson, signing the delivery note with some unintelligible scrawl that looks like Ruggizosh or Plafftonk, so that the carriers cannot prove delivery, so restores his good humour that he goes off quite happily to do a spot of work in the dahlia beds. Gardening can reform anyone in time.

GALOSHES

I am having a *rapprochement* with galoshes
And some would say this heralds middle age;
Yes, sneering they would say
'Does he always wear *pince-nez*?
Old jossers wore galoshes when ladies' hats were cloches,
Ha! Woollen combinations are this dodderer's next stage!'
Well, let these people snigger
Just because my feet look bigger,
For, colossal in galoshes, they are dry among the sploshes;
A story that won't wash is this notion that galoshes,
So snug at slushy crossings, make a man a sloppy figure.
Oh, crossly, and still crosslier,
I have bought shoes ever costlier
Which, still quite new, let water through before I've crossed
    the street:
There's nothing manly, I repeat,
In always having cold wet feet;
Galoshlessness is foolishness when sharply slants the sleet –
And I utterly refuse
The expression 'overshoes',
To make galoshes posher I would scorn this feeble ruse.
The word 'galosh' is strong, not weak,
It comes from *kalopous*, the Greek
For 'cobbler's last', and thus it's classed with hero times
    antique.
Come, Muse, through slush and sleet dry-footed with me
    trip so
That I may praise galoshes in a *kalopous* calypso.

Oh, when swishing buses splash.
And the rush-hour masses clash
When it's marshy as molasses, how galoshes cut a dash!
It makes me quite impassioned
When they're dubbed unsmart, old-fashioned –
(For such, by gosh, the bosh is that's talked about galoshes)
Since the very finest leather
Is outsmarted altogether
By the classy, glossy polish of galoshes in such weather.

Come, galoshers, be assertive,
Drop that air discreet and furtive!
Let galosh shops' stocks be lavish
With designs and hues that ravish –
Men's galoshes black and British, but for ladies colours
    skittish
(And galoshes could make rings
Round those silly plastic things
Which tie up with clumsy strings)
Let us all have this *rapprochement* with galoshes
And see what health and happiness it brings!

MEMO. GET EDUCATED

There is a curious wakefulness about autumn, in spite of the vague melancholy of its weather. This equinoctial balance between winter and summer is a moment of reality between two dreams. In summer the rapt contemplation of bright Being makes in each of us a little Athens, where the West first took shape, where singing marble columns in the clear sunlight echo the pristine mental structure wrought against Nothing. Seen from this light, this clarity, the winter seems a dream, a misty chaos, a barbarous Ultima Thule.

But in winter we mirror the westward move of civilization. In the sharp, cold air, we raise the Gothic cities, teeming and practical. We despise the siesta; only dimly do we remember our ancestry in sun-baked Sumeria. We have triumphed over the eastern torpor, over the sunny lethargy which settled over the first glories and made them easy prey for the barbarians. To us now, summer is a dream, of life suspended in shimmering empty heat.

But in autumn we are half-way, we balance both dreams. This is when the academic year begins, when thought and reality meet. In autumn we make a new attack on meaning, whether we are freshmen enrolling or amateur actors waving our unlearnt scripts under the ugly lampshades. This wakefulness, this new starting, takes different forms with different people; and with me it takes the form of resolving to enter on some vast winter reading task.

Every winter this picture forms in my mind, of myself in an armchair, with a green reading lamp; exploring the uttermost echoing halls of the intellect; while the wet

73

trees roar outside, I will become more and more real. . . .

The only trouble is, I don't know where to start. There are at least three major difficulties. First of all, *what* shall I read? Shall I buy a set of Proust? I am tired of knowing only that he wrote in a cork-lined room and is beautifully sad about the second-handness of adult experience. I want to read about this Swann. On the other hand, what a splendid thing it would be to read the whole of Gibbon, to hear the grand surf of history beating in sonorous eighteenth-century cadences – and to get those Antonine emperors sorted out once for all.

But wait a minute, is not this a great chance to read some of the English novelists who existed before Jane Austen – to be able to add to a literary conversation some quiet, impressive remark about Fielding, to make one last attempt to read that dreary disjointed stuff about My Uncle Toby?And what do I know about Spenser? What a terrifying blank my mind is about those great French wits, saying imperishable things under the chandeliers. I have seen Mesdames de Sévigné and de Staël, to say nothing of Montesquieu (I like *him*, isn't he the one who admired the British Constitution?) and Montaigne quoted so often that I feel I know all about them; it is only in the autumn that I realize with a shock that I haven't read a single word by any of them. If it weren't for the fact that I *have* read Pascal's *Pensées*, I think I would certainly have a French winter. . . .

This kind of speculation leads to the second difficulty – my Page Fifteen Books. What is the good of all these grand ideas when a glance at my bookshelves gives evidence of similar good intentions years ago. I see, for instance, that I bought *Physics and Philosophy*, by Sir James Jeans, in 1943. I took it to India with me in the Army; I can see where the white ants started nibbling it. But, as happens all too often, I only got to page fifteen, where there is still a sheet of paper on which, long ago, I wrote my only note – 'Descartes said "animal spirits" could change direction of matter'. I simply can't remember the context of that; I shall have to start again.

And here is a fine, resonant-sounding book called *Les Élé-*

ments de la grandeur humaine, par Rodolphe Kassner. I remember buying that in Paris in 1949, intensely aware of the
great anguished Western soul after coming out of the Louvre.
Never read a word of it. Let's have a look, at random. *'Le
démesuré, le chrétien, ne peut se mesurer ni s'accomplir par aucun
acte ... le chrétien, dans un sens effroyable, est né criminel.'*
H'm. Born criminal, eh? But what's it *mean*, a demeasured
Christian? ...

And then there's the third difficulty, the way I can't remember the books I *have* read past Page Fifteen. To look
at my bookshelves is to feel like the pier of a bridge, still and
unchanged while the great dark tide of thought slides past
me. Many times I have tried to be a boat, to sail on to the
infinite sea of knowledge. I read carefully about the Renais-
sance, and three months later it is all just a blur of Guelphs
and Ghibellines. I read St Thomas Aquinas, and in no time
the sharp concepts of Essence, Quantity, and Substance began
to merge imperceptibly into one another. Is this really *my*
note in the margin, saying grandly, 'Newton, force at a distance, begs question?' Did I ever understand it?

Nevertheless, in autumn the thought persists that one day
I shall.

THE CASE OF THE 1,251 BEARDS

There is a faint but ineradicable feeling of silliness about the act of shaving. Man wakes from sleep and nothingness to life and identity, but before he can move about, making his confident statements to the universe, he must, every morning, go through this curious static dance, mopping and mowing to his reflection in the mirror, half ghost and half hairy animal. (I often cut my ear, but this is probably exceptional.) No one really knows what to think about while shaving.

But I know, now. I think, endlessly, about The 1,251 Men. I have been buying a certain kind of shaving cream for years, and I have only just noticed that it says on the carton it 'has been proved in actual tests by 1,251 men, to make beards easier to cut, to give SMOOTHER, MORE COMFORTABLE SHAVES to 3 men out of 4'.

This claim seems to me to have a gentle, wandering vagueness exactly in tune with the consciousness of a man while shaving. It starts off so confidently (*proved, in actual tests*) and ends on such a mild shoulder-shrugging note, admitting that one in four – roughly 313 of these 1,251 men – gruffly denied having had a more comfortable shave, that one warms to the manufacturers straight away.

If one tries to imagine this test carried out in the usual way, with casual interviews or house-to-house calls, one soon runs into difficulties. One sees the market research boys drawing up a list of eighteen subtle questions ('1. Why do you shave?'); they prepare 1,251 little cards with slots for age-group, profession, income, and even sex (although of course the survey is only of men). They send out their most experienced interviewers. But those neat academic plans are soon upset by the untidy realities of life. At nearly all the houses called on the man, of course, is out at work. If he is at home it is usually an unshaven tough in vest and trousers who growls ''op off, mate. I only shave Sat'dys.'

They try calling before breakfast, when the man *is* shaving, but the children crowd in, round-eyed, the cards become smeared with marmalade. They finally abandon the house-to-house method when their 403rd subject, a waspish little man who has entered 'Professor of Logic' against *Profession* on his card, snaps, 'Yes, yes, I quite see the need for some kind of empirical verification. But kindly define your terms. Smoother and more comfortable than what? Than other shaving creams? Than an electric razor? Than *pumice stone*? And have you standardized the hardness of the water?'

No, surely the whole thing was at once more genial and more controlled. One sees all these 1,251 men being tested simultaneously, at some special function. It would be perfectly ethical to choose a place where the water is soft; and this in England means the north-west, away from chalk and limestone formations. On a summer Saturday two special trains, one from London and one from the Midlands, pull into the station of a pretty little Lake District town. These trains are full of bearded men. A huge marquee has been set up in a verdant park, between the grey stone houses and the sweeping hills. A fleet of coaches takes the bearded men to it.

First they are entertained to lunch, there are welcome speeches and photographs, a band plays musical-comedy selections on a stage decorated with hydrangeas. Then the tests begin; fifty men at a time, at a row of special wash-basins. But although officials in white coats with armbands saying TESTER scurry about like sheepdogs, there is something in the atmosphere, half-way between a flower show and an Army reunion, that makes it happily impossible to coordinate things.

The public address system crackles with announcements: 'If your card shows Test Number Five will you please report to the basins NOW': but they are only half heard above the laughter at the bar, where beer bottles and crumpled card-board plates lie on the trampled grass. Knots of laughing men, with that extraordinary air of having known each other all their lives that will be familiar to anyone who has ever joined the Army with a large intake, gather in the canvassy twilight; occasionally a summer breeze slaps the walls of the marquee against the poles; bursts of applause can be heard from an impromptu cricket match that has developed outside.

Some of the bearded men are already in the middle dist-ance, walking along the path by the clear tumbling river with local girls. Others, watching their cronies actually doing the tests at the wash-basins, encourage them with cries of 'Hack it off, Ginger!' And some of them, observing the chinless, naked effect produced, have second thoughts about under-going the test at all.

For whatever reason, in the end only three out of four men give positive results. But somehow the genial makers don't seem to mind. Nor do I.

TRICERATOPIC

Birmingham Museum and Art Gallery Committee decided today to buy the fossilized skull of a triceratops from the American Museum of Natural History for about £700. At present there are only two in Britain, and Birmingham hopes to have the third early next year. The skull, six feet in length, weighs nearly half a ton. It was dug up in Nevada. The triceratops was a mild-mannered, plant-eating dinosaur, looking something like a rhinoceros, although it had three horns and a bony frill to protect its neck
– *The Times*

In Brum beat the drum from the rooferatops
And trumpet our treasure, the triceratops;
Edgbastodon! Here's something more than a mastodon!
Moseley! A mammal with bony frills plastered on!
A rhino but nicer – a triceratops
Solely subsisting on cereal crops.
Curator! Send parties to Pole or Equator
And nothing you'll find with a charm that is greater;
In Stechford and Shifnal they'll shutter their shops
And stream in to stare at your triceratops,
Tourists from buses, from planes and from ships,
Tricycle tourists with trouseroclips
Will see your museum and clamour in chorus
The Midlands have more than a megalosaurus,
They'll fight for a sight of your triceratops,
You'll have to get more motorcycleocops –

And further we fit you with featherocaps,
How did you diddle the dollarogaps,
The treasurytypes with their stopperostops
On transferable sterling for triceratops?

Preposterous posers will pester posterity
Probing our present prevailing austerity,
Trying to square with the goldreservedrops
Such largesse of lolly for triceratops;
'Perhaps,' they'll opine, 'not in total eclipse
Were men who acquired, with such pocketadips,
A *third* skull for England, now rich to infinity,
Possessing a triceratopian trinity.'

So triple the tipple in claretocups
(Or if you're teetotal, in teaserocups)
Print pressfuls of praise, pulling out all the stops
And pray, sirs, a toast to THE TRICERATOPS.

THE BIRDS THAT NEVER WERT

When I learnt at school about the Roman augurs basing state decisions on the flight of birds I used to think this was a pretty fey idea for such a practical, bridge-building sort of people. But the more I look at birds the more I see what the Romans meant. Of all non-human creation, the birds give the most powerful impression of being up to something, of *knowing* something. In their quick, giggling, hopping, jerking, twitching, twittering way they seem to have a direct, intuitive contact with the secret of life. We have to get there by careful and disciplined thought, we have to wrestle with time – and even then we can't be sure of that sudden liberation, that sudden flash of truth and ecstasy; we can't *make* it happen. But birds live there all the time.

Quick, quick, said the bird.

Birds are not single, either. They know whatever it is they know together. They are not allowed to tell us (unless we are in the St Francis class), but they know about us too, they swoop mimbling and tweaking at us, turning away in a perfect swift curve, with a hint of message for us; but it is too quick. Of course, they don't know it all, they just know the part we don't know, and vice versa; the ones who know *everything* are a combination of man and bird – the angels.

Birds and men live in two parallel real worlds, and they, in their skittering, indirect way, are just as interested in the point where these two worlds meet as we are. In towns they reflect our organization; starlings form themselves into vast urban regiments, pigeon housewives go shopping. In the country they adopt a casual, rural attitude. They come into my garden for drinks in the evening; many of them live in my house, in the roof, I can hear them stamping about in the roof. Birds I have never seen before – birds made of check tweed, of silk, birds with beards, big brown birds like bookmakers, come and surprise my ignorance.

I know this is not just a subjective reaction, because I have bought *The Observer's Book of Birds* (not *the Observer*, it's published by Frederick Warne, and jolly good too). This book is by a serious bird expert, Mr S. Vere Benson, who knows about things like the Little Stint, the Knot, the Brambling, the Siskin. And the picture of bird life that emerges is even closer to ours than I had imagined.

Who would have thought, for instance, that the skylark 'does not hop, but walks or runs'? It makes all that profuse strain of art seem not quite so un-premeditated; one sees the skylark walking about on the ground trying out a few arias, like a singer pacing the corridors in the Albert Hall before going on. Some birds actually *growl* (e.g. the Razorbill: 'a grunt or growling note'), and that certainly brings them closer. Or take the Fulmar – an unknowable bird if ever there was, I should have thought, wheeling out of Atlantic snow-storms; but the book says 'a silent bird except at the colonies, where a low cackling is heard as the birds gape at one another with strange gestures'. It sounds just like life in Delhi in the old days.

Perhaps the most poetic, quasi-human, yet *other* life of all is lived by the Manx Shearwater, which 'comes into land at breeding places at night, with weird cooing cries and wails, and shuffles to tunnels from which sepulchral voices coo "kuk-kuk-hoo-coo"'. With a little rearrangement this is pure Tennyson:

> in breeding haunts at night
> And weird in tunnels, cooing cries and wails
> Sepulchral husky voices coo *'hoo coo'*
> Under long glories of the winter moon.

None of these are the birds I actually want to look up. I

get diverted on to these fascinating creatures, that growl and shuffle in tunnels, while the ones I am looking up fly away. I can't help feeling that the birds we have aren't in the book anyway. We have the Telephone Bird, which makes a noise exactly like a telephone bell heard through three doors. We rush to answer it, the phone is silent, it was that bird again. The Telephone Bird is a resident, 8 in. long, and dances at night in old pipes. Then we have the Garage Bird, found all over southern England in garages where *convertible* cars are kept, with perishable hoods. Even the novice bird-watcher can detect their presence, for his car looks as though it were kept permanently in Trafalgar Square. They live in garages in colonies of twenty or thirty. They eat brown paper and Scotch Tape, at least they do in my garage. I put up sheets of heavy brown paper, hanging underneath the nests, to protect my hood. The next morning it was lying in strips on the car or hanging from the roof. The Garage Birds, which are very small seagulls, and their fledgelings, which hatch out in *September* and look like small vultures, were sitting on a beam, eating brown paper and growling. I have an idea they drink paraffin, too. The tap on my paraffin drum is always dribbling when I come into the garage, and there is a Garage Bird fluttering drunkenly between the drum and the window. It is hard to see whether they like me or not. They must know that if there were no men there would be no garages for them to live in, and no paraffin. But they always try to make me jump, they flitter just too close to my ears in the dark garage. I wish they would go and shuffle in some tunnels. I don't think I like birds quite as close as this.

LOAD OF HOGGIN

It was only just light (and it gets light an hour earlier in the country) when the front-door bell rang and there was a man saying tersely, 'Load of hoggin.' For a moment I couldn't think who he was, or what hoggin was – indeed, I'm never quite sure who *I* am at that hour in the morning.

Hoggin, now what could it be? A kind of rude cider? A fertilizer made from pigs' ears and washed leaves? Some sort of intermediate product in brewing or tanning? Some sort of intermediate product in brewing or tanning ('the sparge-arms scrape off the hoggin, which is then pressed into these giant kieves')?

A huge, square, high-sided lorry stood outside in the mist; the kind of lorry you follow for miles, it bears some name like FRANK COGGS, sandy mud dribbles out of it at the corners – and then I remembered, hoggin is a sort of gravel. I had ordered it for my front path.

I had planned to smarten up the front, at least; I had to choose between making a large, diffuse impression at the back, creating a tiny, vestigial human spoor in the wilderness – a little bit of lawn, a cultivated plot of maize won from the jungle – and making a real garden at the front.

In fact the front became an obsession, one thing led to another. I planted hundreds of bulbs. I attacked it with the misplaced frenzy of the urban gardener, although in my heart I know you can't win like this, you have to attack the country when it isn't looking. You must be born in it, you crouch slyly over your handlebars, you have sacks containing moles

84

or voles, bang goes your mysterious gun in the foggy twilight; you know what the owls are saying.

I didn't even know that bulbs have a top and a bottom until one of these bicycle men pointed it out; half my tulips will come up in Australia. I made some marvellous lawn edges; I painted the railings white. For two pins I'd have had a flagstaff and some whitewashed bricks. Then I saw that the front path, just old pebbles and mud, wouldn't live up to the surrounding splendour; and the man with the bicycle said: 'Ah, you want to get a load of hoggin.'

It was a huge load, filling the lorry right to the top. It was four cubic yards. The builder whom I first asked for this hoggin said he wasn't allowed to deliver it at all, and the actual hoggin people weren't allowed to deliver *less* than four cubic yards. There was some confused reason for this, all about A and B licences. Indeed, the hoggin, binding shingle, and washed sand world is more complicated, in fact exciting, than I had imagined. On the back of the note I had to sign for my load it said:

FOR THE USE OF INSPECTORS ONLY

This Conveyance Note having been produced to me at (place)   at (time)   on the
        day of   19......, I found the same to contain materially incorrect statements, particulars of which are as follows:

– followed by a lot of Notes, all fatalistically expecting trouble. So *that's* why those lorries are forever lurching suddenly down side-roads, they have spied the Hoggin Inspector in his car, and the chase is on. It is like smugglers and revenue men in the eighteenth century, although heaven knows who would want to smoggle hugg – to smuggle hoggin. Perhaps it all belongs to the Crown, like swans, and since half England seems to be shakily founded on the Bunter Pebble Beds these Inspectors are constantly tracking down illegal operators.

It was such a big load that I couldn't decide where to have it dumped. After fruitless, panting attempts by the driver and me to pull up the railings I saw it would have to be outside the garage. I had the foresight to get my car out first. Immediately it began to rain, the weather began its ceaseless attack on my hood. The driver tipped up his lorry. A vast mound of soggy sand, with a pebble here and there, cascaded across the entrance.

After a hurried breakfast I got busy. I wheeled barrowful after barrowful. At midday, after twenty-nine barrows, the vast heap seemed hardly diminished at all. The path was littered with awful giant molehills. Plodding with my barrow, I felt like a Chinese coolie making an airstrip in some sodden rice-field. As a rest from the exhausting wheelbarrow I raked this dreary hoggin and tried to roll it. The roller simply sank in it, it was like rolling mud. It *was* rolling mud, that's what hoggin is: it's mud.

I telephoned my builder, he sent me two men with bicycles to help me, we just managed to clear a way through the hoggin for my car as darkness fell. Now, the stuff on the path gets wetter and wetter, there are parts that simply suck one down. The laundry man who, surprisingly, materializes out of the dark fields at about eight in the evening, was white and shaken.

'I thought I'd stepped into wet concrete,' he said. I didn't tell him it was a quicksand, but I shouldn't be surprised if there are cries for help one night, and I have to go out with ropes and ladders to rescue some unfortunate victim, like Carver Doone in the bog. I don't think I like hoggin.

ONCE BITTEN

Perhaps one of the reasons why talking to dogs has reached, in the twentieth century, a degree of conviction never known before is that man instinctively knows himself to be neither the highest nor the lowest intelligence in the universe; and now that the broodingness has gone out of our earth and the voice of Pan is silent, there is an even greater poignancy in the curious intelligence, so like and so unlike our own, that looks out of the eyes of dogs, bringing a hint of the Other, of the vast wordless articulation of Nature, into the most sterile blocks of flats.

Talking to dogs is one of the few acts of faith still made nowadays. 'Come along, darling, we must get back in case the plumber comes,' I heard a woman say to her dog. She was an intelligent-looking woman, who would, presumably, have admitted that the concept 'plumber', or even merely the overtones of the word 'darling', are far beyond a dog's comprehension. Yet she sent out this human message, not simply as an absurd subjective statement into the void – a *mad* statement; she made an unquestioned act of faith, that she was somehow communicating with that subfusc limbo of the intelligence where animals have their being.

For myself, I am rarely capable of this act of faith. I like dogs, I have had dogs myself, but there is something in me that stops me from talking about plumbers to them; and they know it. Their knowing it does not necessarily make them dislike me in the way that some creatures – bees, for instance – dislike me (I like bees, too. I talk romantically about the Fourth Georgic. But when friends show me their bees they simply sting my head. Some fearful, Martian rumour of cold, irrational hate goes round the hive. Fall in the guard. It's Jennings, the hive-wrecker, the bee-hater. Die for the Fatherland. Sting his head). No, dogs simply behave *differently* towards me.

Often they get hysterical. I go to a party at a house where they have a rather soppy boxer, who jumps up at each new arrival. But he quietens down, and when we start playing an acting game he remains perfectly quiet until it is my turn. Then he gets hysterical. He shadow-boxes with me, I have to laugh him off as if he were a drunken friend whom I wished to quieten without offending. He knows I am worried about this act of faith, he is trying shock tactics from his side.

Of course, dogs (and bees) are in much more direct contact with the world-store of love and hate than we are, with our clouds of bodiless words, and there are dramatic, critical moments when even I make this act of faith. The other day, lunching in a pub, I asked for the telephone and was directed to the end of a brown corridor; and there was an awful Alsatian, baring its teeth at me (I'd like to see anybody breathe down *its* nose to win its confidence). I heard myself saying, 'It's all right, boy, I'm only telephoning.' *Boy*, I said *boy*. True, I spoke partly for the benefit of the barmaid who was passing with a tray, hoping to be drawn into the obviously peaceful relationship between her and this terrible dog – but also partly to the dog itself, as an act of faith.

It is always more confusing when human beings are involved as well. I was once walking in Kensington Gardens, in that slack week-day late afternoon when the earth gives off a dull light from inside, and a man feels curiously alien, oppressed by the heavy, quiescent life-force of women, and children out of school, and dogs. There was a commotion by the Round Pond, caused by a fight between a boxer and a spaniel. The boxer had the spaniel by the neck and was scientifically trying to drown it. I had read in a dog-lovers' magazine that most people just grin foolishly at a dog-fight, a legacy from the bear-baiting and cock-fighting days, or else they sadistically throw pepper or use a stick, whereas the correct way is to hold the uppermost dog by tail and collar and 'turn it gently through 180 degrees.'

I tried this on the boxer and it turned its head briefly and bit two fingers to the bone. So I got a cane from a boy who was fishing and hit it very hard. It immediately let go of the spaniel and walked away, with a small sigh.

Quite a large and sympathetic crowd gathered and vocally expressed solicitude over the wound, and various plans of assistance were being made while I, unspoken to, was walking away. It wasn't my wound they were discussing, but the spaniel's.

PATTER SONG

Mutters and Natters. These twinlike villages are ideal centres for a quiet holiday. They lie a short distance apart on a plateau overlooking Innsbruck – a good starting-point for local excursions. There is a chairlift to the Muttereralm, and bathing facilities at the Natterersee. At Mutters you can stay at the Hotel Muttererhof, where our Hostess resides. At Natters there are the Gasthof Sonnenheim, and the Gasthof Eichhof, where a 15-day holiday can be had for £25 7s. od. – *from Messrs Dean & Dawson's Holiday Guide.*

In flatters and bedsitters let us shut up all the shutters
Leaving fritters on the platters, quitting blotters on the desk;
The only word that matters or that anybody utters
Is *holiday*; it scatters us to places picturesque.
For the hatters or the fitters who like fish all fried in batters,
For strutters on smart cutters in the waters of the Bay,
For rotters, or their betters who have worked themselves to tatters,
How it glitters, does the prospect of a chance to Get Away!
How the guide-books lie in clutters, how map-plotters get the jitters,
As the writers on each spot assure the flitters it's the best!
Shall we chatter on a terrace, sipping Spanish gin-and-bitters,
Or potter on the *trottoir* at a little place near Brest?

But surely no one totters off to Natters or to Mutters
Where every epiglottis utters words that are not kind,
Words all titters or all stutters, not a word that parsnip butters;
Where knitters sit and batter reputations out of mind.
In Natters each one mutters and in Mutters each one natters,
Of scandal they're begetters, they are putters-out of tales;

And setters-out on holiday should really be congratters
If they choose not Mutters, Natters, but some quiet place in
  Wales –
Ah, we were wrong! There life is a song
As up in the chairlift one rides;
Majestic and calm is the Muttereralm;
And gay, where the Hostess resides,
Is the Muttererhof, where one lives like a toff
And contemplates Innsbruck below;
And gay, very gay, is the Natterersee
As bathing enthusiasts know;
Come, nothing else matters! Let's hie us to Natters
Or Mutters-ward straight let us go!

THE SNIFFLE GROUP

Like many news stories which suddenly fizzle out (did that man ever open Walsingham's tomb, was there a faded parchment inside saying *It was mee all ye time, tee hee. C. Marlowe?* Who was Princess Ira's *husband?* Are they all happy in Guatemala now?) the one about that research centre for the common cold leaves a vague question mark in the mind. People were asked to go as guinea-pigs, weren't they; they were offered a free holiday in lovely country if they would accept a few injections which might, or might not, give them colds? One imagined a lot of huts dotted about the parkland of some ex-mansion in Wiltshire, and scientists in white coats looking on despairingly as the volunteers, healthier than ever after their injections, borrowed the centre's Land Rover for a day's dissipation in Salisbury or Devizes.

For there was a general impression that there is a baffling, elusive quality about the cold virus. Now, I can't help feeling that this is because the cold differs from all other illnesses in not being an individual affliction at all, with definite germs, or a definite quantity of virus, in individual people. We need a new conception. There is really only one cold in the country – the *common* cold in fact. It is to be thought of as a huge sort of cloud with an awful glooming face, as a subtly subsisting ether, almost a kind of ectoplasmic sponge, hovering and wandering over England, expanding, drawing in on itself, concentrating or dissipating in a loose, not always logical correspondence with the weather; a National Cold, like the National Debt.

The ordinary experience of life shows us that there is a

married cold, much more diffuse and indefinite than the bachelor cold; and there is a further step to the family cold, a strange wispy thing that sometimes lurks in cupboards, sometimes wanders vaguely about the house, making children cough in the night and demand sticky yellow medicine just when you thought it was all over; a cold that never actually resides in one person. It is but a step from this to the notion of the universal, the common cold: The Cold.

When my friend Harblow came to stay with us recently, he very nearly went away again the moment he discovered that our family cold had come out of the cupboard. Harblow has monumental bachelor colds, ten days long, full of *angst* and temperatures. He attracts the attention of The Cold, as a nervous outpost attracts the enemy by wild firing. For he buys lozenges; he is always fishing out little tins containing pastilles on the borderline between folly, frivolous sweets and serious medicine. They are a sort of charm; he pops them into his mouth in the Tube, in bed, even in church.

Some carry stern warnings that they must not be taken at less than three-hourly intervals, or even 'as recommended by physicians' (although Harblow eats them all the time, I half expect to see him keel over or go into a coma). Some merely advise the consumer to 'place one on the tongue and allow to dissolve slowly in the mouth' (as opposed to what? Frying them in batter? Threading them on a string and hanging them round the neck?). Some are ancient remedies, made by Wise Women or monks from herbs. Others give an impressive-looking scientific formula, always with glycerine 0.8 per cent. Some are black, some red, some yellow. Some are little more than fruit drops, others excoriate the tongue, and purge the very lungs with strong acrid whiffs, destroying the taste of food for hours afterwards. I have seen Harblow go into a chemist's shop to buy dyspepsia tablets, to cure dyspepsia brought on by eating too many throat tablets. In our local chemist's he discovered some new ones: it said on the paper in the box: *The pastille that was made for one man – the great Caruso.*

'They're marvellous,' he said. 'I felt that ominous tickle

at the back of the throat last night, but I took a couple of these and it's gone completely today.' He went out for a walk by himself, I suspect to try out *Donna è mobile* in the woods. We didn't hear him sing, although I was reminded of the old days in the Army when I heard him getting up. Harblow is a man you always *hear* getting up. He gargles – and he doesn't just say *aaaa-ah* to gargle, he shouts it. He has one of those razors that have to be rolled up and down in a sharpening device, *crack, crack, crack* it goes at about 6.30 a.m. (fellow-patients in hospital always seem to have them too) – and one hears the tinkle of endless little bottles and jars and mugs and mirrors and tins, with which he used to adorn the most temporary tent; and the violent splooshing washing, and the half-hour-long shaving …

Actually he did get a mild sniffle, probably his first mild cold for years. He thinks it was the Caruso pastilles that saved him from a worse one. But I know it was because he was simply entered into vaguely by our family cold.

DROP IN FOR BILLIARDS

The Viscount dropped gently down over the extraordinary jumble of townlets, thin woods, and many-shaped ponds filled with chemically green or muddily yellow water with which London seems, from the air, to be surrounded for thirty miles. I was home again, but still completely isolated. There was none of the strange twilight of change that one feels in other forms of travel. These million grey roofs, these sunset-reflecting windows, these dead ponds, did not speak to the traveller. There were none of the subtle changes of, say, a road journey to the West Country, where the softening horizons call out, 'Stop, do not ignore us, we also are England'; where the towns become more and more individual, strange, London-free; where there are comfortable shops crammed with slightly old-fashioned tin toys, shops that contain rubber boots for farmers and festoon their doorways with carpet slippers looking as if they were growing there, like bunches of bananas; where people move calmly in the soft, moist air, lapped about with unheard passacaglias of airy music, a dreamy Atlantic music washing round their old grey towns.

Nor, as I came in by air, did strange, half-read notices flash across my vision like omens. (Once driving through some sad conurbation, coming to a part where there was a barely perceptible intensification of like, like the nucleus of an amoeba – a bus shelter, a fried-fish shop, a public lavatory – I read on a high blank wall, above a sad shop stuffed with pink vests, THE PARIS HOUSE. Long ago, some Edwardian signwriter had enlivened this dull place with those vaunting words. But on whose instruction? Who, who had this impossible dream of elegance among the low brick houses?)

But when the Viscount was down to a thousand feet or so I looked out again. And there beneath me, among the anonymous suburbs, was this hugely painted word on a roof:

BILLIARDS

Instantly the table-model, impersonal landscape below became alive, mysterious, human, full of half-understood messages calling out to the traveller, even the air traveller. Somewhere, down in that suburb (where *was* it, though, Acton? Muswell Hill? Harlesden?) some billiard-hall owner – a rotund, balding little man in shirtsleeves, with a little moustache and humorous round face, chewing a cigar, known to everyone as Pop – had conceived this marvellous idea of advertising to the skies. He had hired painters to go up on his roof and paint the huge letters, ten feet long, invisible to people down in the street. First in the field, long before the professional agencies had thought of great horizontal hoardings laid out under the air lanes, Pop had confidently made this bid for an international clientele.

One longs to know whether it worked. Were the locals, potting quietly away in the smoke-laden, green-reflecting light, cross or thrilled when the doors burst open and tables were hastily booked by babbling passengers from Aero-lineas Argentinas, Alitalia, Sabena, K.L.M., and even Flugfelag (Iceland), giving the drab hall the gay, cosmopolitan air of a casino?

Or is it all terribly sad? Was this notice on the roof a last desperate attempt by Pop to get custom for his empty hall – its old patrons dying off, the younger ones staying at home with the television? Did he stand sadly in the doorway of this hall, looking down the empty, rainswept street, perplexed and hurt in his simple mind that no one had responded to his advertisement; not realizing that even if people wanted to come they couldn't know where his hall *was*, from the air?

Or is it a more private and professional affair? Is it for the pilots and crews? Is 'Pop's' an internationally known rendezvous? Do the splendid captains, in their dark glasses, as they walk to their great machines waiting on the blinding tarmac on the other side of the world, say, 'Cheerio, see you at Pop's'? Is billiards, calmest of all games that can be played while still actually standing up, a favourite airman's game? Billiards, with its restful green table and little clicking noises, after the tense hours in the throbbing cabin, the needle flickering below the red line, the anxiety about No. 4 engine high over the tumbling ocean?

Who knows? It doesn't really matter what the ground says to us while we're up there so long as it says *something*.

THE TROPICAL SUIT

Perhaps today tourism has replaced tribal migration, *Völker-wanderungen*, the restless, instinctive movements of popula-tion that were the ground-swell of history.

Seen from the airport bus humming through fainting airs, over a parched landscape, to some white southern city, the ancient symbolic horizons take on a fearful novelty (shall we get out, now, and walk straight over them, with our overnight briefcases?). For a moment we feel again the otherness of the world, its invitation and bright promise; a huge thirst clamours within us, we shall know the unknowable. The earth will speak to us.

But just because we *are* individuals, weighed down by the strange bathos of human clay – or perhaps because we are only tourists – we keep returning from these vast, nameless thoughts to trivial personal worries. In the heavy afternoon, when the locals retire behind white walls, and we hear their distant radio music, we vaguely want tea. We worry about postcards, we buy useless foreign ball-point pens. We count our money. We fill the interstices of the day with needless trips to our hotel rooms.

My own particular worry, as a tourist, and as one occasion-ally sent or invited on exotic journalistic jobs, is clothes. Recently, for instance, I was invited on what amounted to a day-trip to Tangier. Naturally, I wanted to go. But I didn't want to be worried, under the palm trees, by itchy, hot, flannel trousers; for my lightest suit is of grey flannel. Nor did I want to buy a tropical suit for one day in Tangier.

In the end I compromised with a second-hand one. It was

in cream linen, and it cost only four guineas. I felt rather pleased as I looked at the sixteen me's in the little fitting-cubicle. I looked like the Manila City Council, or a group photograph of Lieutenant Pinkerton's brother officers in *Madame Butterfly*. True, it seemed a bit loose-fitting. But then, it was a tropical suit.

I began to have my first doubts when I tried it on again at home. It *was* loose-fitting. I noticed now, also, that the lapels were old-fashioned and short, in the style of the early thirties, instead of long and meeting over a single button. This coat had three buttons. A laundry label said *Hammond*, tersely. I began to feel a pygmy in the clothes of this Hammond – a tough, red-faced man with short-cropped grey hair; heavily built, running a little to fat after a muscular, pig-sticking youth; Hammond, retired after a lifetime build-ing railways and bridges in the tropics; Hammond, reading *Blackwood's* in a wicker chair....

I didn't dare appear at Waterloo Air Terminal as a pseudo-Hammond. I wrapped the suit in brown paper. I thought I would change at Gibraltar. By Gibraltar I had discovered that all the other journalists had suits which, while lighter than my grey flannel, were unmistakably *them*, part of their ordinary wardrobes. However, it was too late now. It was hot, and the flannel was itchy.

My emergence from the B.E.A. manager's office where I had changed caused a mild sensation. I reminded one journa-list of some rajah he had known. I said shamelessly, 'I've had this old thing for years, and it is so comfortable.' (It was, except that the trousers kept slipping down.)

We took off on the twenty-minute last lap to Tangier. We sailed over the white city, we stepped out at the quiet little country airport. There were Berbers with enormous hats, and thin brown horses; bright green patches of cultivation, and far stony hills. Africa, *Africa*, I wanted to start straight off and walk down to Kano, the walled city of Nigeria. But we were all driven off in an enormous Chrysler, to marvellous meals and swimming and cocktails and polo and bazaars and cool Moorish courtyards. Occasionally (at the polo, for instance) I thought about my suit, and noticed that it was getting more and more rumpled, like a pair of pyjamas.

All the same, I didn't want to start the homeward journey in my grey flannel. At 2.30 a.m. of the morning we were due to leave I remembered I had lost the original brown paper, and I had planned to change back again in the aeroplane. I lifted the bedside telephone.

'*Allo,*' said a thick Arab voice.

'*Est-ce-que vous avez un morceau de papier brun?*' I said. The voice was silent. '*Non,*' I went on wildly, '*pas un morceau, avez-vous* BEAUCOUP *de papier brun? C'est pour mon taille.*' (Was that the word for suit? It was 2.30 a.m. and it had been quite a party.) '*Je veux changer dans l'avion, et il faut faire un package*' (that didn't sound right either).

'*Pardon?*' said the voice.

I tried Spanish. '*Yo quiero papel bruno.*' (Heavens, had I said 'I love brown paper', not 'I want it'?) '*Papel bruno.* PAPEL.'

'*Ah, si,*' said the voice, '*café.* You want coffee?'

I felt sure this kind of thing never happened to Hammond. But then he was not a tourist.

GANGSTER GONGSTER

SINGAPORE, February 25 – The booming gongs and clashing cymbals which have been a feature of Chinese funerals for centuries will no longer be heard in Singapore. The police have forbidden them as part of their campaign against Chinese secret societies. A police spokesman said many gangsters were registered as funeral musicians. Fights had broken out in the past when members of rival societies tried to outgong each other, and then discarded their gongs for bottles and knives – *The Times*

Gongster bangster! Gangster bongster!
Suzie Wongster! Heartless mongster!
Get thee hengst! The gong thou bangst
Adds public woe to private angst;
Seemly grief is what belongster
Funerals, not Tong war, Tongster!
Cursed the cymbals that thou clangst,
Get thee hengst! We hope thou hangst!

Nor cause woe and angst amongst us
At the weddingst of our youngsters;
Ill the omens that thou bringst!
Inauspicious songs thou singst!
When young bachelors wed spingsters,
Putting rings on pretty fingsters,
Weddings from the start are jinxed
If to bong and clang thou thinkst!

Badman bongster! Gunman gangster!
Sacrilegious *sturm-und-drangster*!
Music's very soul thou wrongst
When thy rivals thou outgongst –
Rivalry mere discord bringster

Brassist, woodwindman or stringster!
Brutal bangster! Ghastly gongster!
(Singaporester or Hong Kongster)
Learn, ere funeral gang thou bongst,
Life is short, but art is longst.

BALLYBURBLING

Ballymackleduff, Derryfubble, Benburb – *Address of subscriber in Northern Ireland Telephone Directory*

Och, the world was full of grievin', an' when I'd had enough
I packed me bag and set me face towards Ballymackleduff;
White houses nestle there, all far from toil an' trouble
(O the lough an' the sea birds, an' sweet Derryfubble!).
I thought me heart would melt for joy, an' nothin' might
    disturb
The peace that I'd be findin' in beautiful Benburb.

O, the friends of me youth was there to make me comin'
    merry,
First I drank with Mick the Tanner just a mile from Fubble-
    derry
An' Roaring Pat was waitin' in the bar at Mackleben.
'Begod,' says he, 'have one with me'; three jolly Irish men
With all the pints o' porter, the gossip an' the cackle.
'Twas dancin' in the road we was that goes to Berrymackle.

Then up spake Mick the Tanner that was born in Fubble-
    mack:
'The boys at Ballyfubble will be glad to see ye back –
Let's be goin' to O'Reilly's, where the Fiddler of Benbally
An' the Fubblederry Fluter is in his Dancin' Palais
An' the girls from Ferrymackle an' from Bubblefurbyduff
Is doin' all the jiggin' an' the rock-an'-rollin' stuff.'

Ah, hadn't we the time at all at Glubbymacklederry
With all the folk from Grabble an' from Ballygubbleferry

An' Mackledubblegurgle, an' Blubberderryglen
An' the lasses from Duffmackle, an' the rantin' Burble men,
The Squintin' Men from Brackle, an' Mrs Tom Macnally
An' the seven black-haired sisters that live over in Duffbally.

An' wilder came the music from the Fubblederry Flute
An' Mick was drinking Guinness from the Widow Leary's
    boot
An' Roarin' Pat was fightin' with a man from Derryburble
That laid him out and wrote a sign that said DO NOT
    DISTURBLE.

Oh, shut was all the factories, and open all the bars,
There was laughter in the lamplight and kissin' by the stars,
Delight in Derryfubble; and Benburb was full of song;
Ah, Ballymackleduff! Why *did* I stay away so long?

TO BE LEAD OUT LOUD

The Board of Trade recently announced relaxations of the control of trade with China. The following articles, however, are among the exports still prohibited:

Gravity hammers having a falling weight of over 10 tons.

Artificial graphite ... having a boron content of one part per million or less.

Ball bearings, bore sizes over 0, including 50 mm., having wobble or parallelism of track to face of ·0003 in.

Gyro-compasses, north-seeking only.

Metals in the form of angles, anodes, bars, billets, blocks, blooms, cakes, castings and forgings, cathodes, channels, circles, discs, dust, flakes, foil, grains, granules, ingots, lumps, pigs, pellets, pipes, plates, powder, pressings and stampings, ribbons, rods, sections, sheets, shapes, shot, slabs, sticks, strips, sponge, tubes, wire ...

Dichlorotetrafluoroethane.

Picric acid.

> Hoolay! Hoolay! The Board of Tlade
> Lelaxing all lestliction
> Lushes to our countly's aid,
> Leducing cause of fliction;
> Now at last they lealize
> China wants machinely;
> The past of silks and dlagons dies,
> We've bloken with it cleanly.
> Please dispatch us as per note
> A hundled thousand tlactors,
> A floating clane (complete with float;
> State Load Conversion Factors);
> Lailway engines we lequire,
> Looms and genelators,
> Nuts and bolts and copper wire –

Impelialistic tlaitors!
Wire you still lefuse to sell
Or metal glains or plessings,
Glanules, lods, with which to swell
Our economic blessings,
Pigs and libbons, stlips to weld
And speed our levolution,
Lumps and pellets – all withheld
To spite our land Confucian!
On gylo-compass seeking north
And monstlous hammers (glavity)
Your hollid interdict goes forth
With bourgeois, base deplavity.
How can China take her place
Among ball-bealing users
When palallels of tlack to face
Of fineness, you lefuse us?

How industlial lace be lun
If glaphite with less bolon
Than a millionth part in one
Is all you let us call on –
How fulfilled our Five Year Plan?
Without dichlolotetla –
Fluoloethane, how can man
Bleak tylant's bonds, *et cetela*?
Lacking piclic acid, how
Can we a New Dawn usher?

We'll make it all ourselves, since now
We've had a low with Lussia.

GENES WITH LIGHT BROWN HAIR

In recent correspondence about 'Tom, the illiterate boy', it always seemed to be assumed that this classification is made once and for all in childhood.

Now this does not work in my case. I could read before I went to school, and I got on fine while I was there. It is only now that I am beginning to feel like Tom, sitting at the back with a foolish smile as the incomprehensible words sail over his head. And, oddly enough, one of the chief reasons for this is the Pelican Library.

I am forever buying Pelicans. There is an element of challenge about these little blue paperbacks that cannot be ignored. Here, laid out specifically for 'the ordinary reader', is a vast distillation of knowledge, scientific as well as literary. Somewhere there is a kind of consortium of the best brains in the country, carefully and brilliantly planning the education of the complete twentieth-century man. Behind every Pelican one sees these figures, noble, withdrawn, betrousered, with high domelike foreheads, standing in deep thoughtful attitudes (indeed, was there not a painting of them all by Rodrigo Moynihan?) in some celestial common-room. It is always an anti-climax to observe that the books actually come from Harmondsworth, Middlesex.

In a quiet part of the bookshop, away from the gaudy best-sellers, the silent rows of Pelican books attune one to effort and virtue. This is what printing is *for*. Look, here, Leibniz in a nutshell. . . .

But by page 16 in most Pelican books I feel just like Tom. I don't seem to *start* right. I never get a clear picture of the

units, the counters, the terms. Thus I have been reading the
Pelican *Genetics*, by H. Kalmus. What a miracle the whole
thing is, that one should be like one's father, only different.
I must find out about these marvellous genes. But it seems
that genes are particles in chromosomes, which are structures
in cell nuclei; there are also hormones and zygotes and
gametes, to say nothing of molecules and proteins. In the end
I see them all as a lot of very small dots, all subtly different
in some way that escapes me. I stare at a diagram under which
it says, 'Equal numbers of non-crossovers, single crossovers
on the left, single crossovers on the right, and double cross-
over chromatids result. (Redrawn from Sturtevant and
Beadle, 1940.)'

And slowly, inevitably, the Tom-feeling begins to steal over
me. Just as Tom's mind, baffled by the half-understood
phrases on some endless drowsy summer afternoon, wanders
off to the woods, to last night's television, to a mole on the
teacher's chin, so do I get diverted by ludicrous inessentials.
Sturtevant, a prim New Englander, in a high rounded collar,
looking like those photographs of Woodrow Wilson: and
Beadle – well, a beadle, with a pink round face ... what an
extraordinary couple, what were they *doing* in 1940?

I know I should try to understand statements like this:

Crossing the homozygous *Gram ram* with *gram gram* will produce
100 per cent *Gram gram* plants, all having broad leaves, whereas
crossing *Gram gram* with *gram gram* will produce about 50 per cent
Gram gram with broad leaves and about 50 per cent *gram gram* plants
with narrow leaves (p. 56).

(Try reading this aloud.) Now, now, let let me me think think,
or Think think....

And then, suddenly, capriciously, I am led off by one of
Mr Kalmus's throwaway lines:

... for instance, Japanese waltzing mice, which run after their
tails, suffer from an abnormality of the inner ear; racehorses are
of a lighter build than carthorses, and red cabbages have ...

Hey, *wait*! Never mind about racehorses and cabbages. Are
there really shops where one could say: 'I want a Japanese

waltzing mouse,' and the man would say 'Yes, sir; male or female?' I do not see it as a female, a kind of geisha mouse. There is a fierce, masculine, hieratic sound about it, as though this mouse were dressed in stiff little silks and brandished a midget sword. How sad to think that these tiny formal antics, admired long ago by courtiers and ladies, are simply due to earache. How sad when, later in *Genetics*, the exotic little animal is 'crossed with an ordinary house mouse' – a slatternly mouse called Doreen born in a shed in Islington, and a great film fan:

JAPANESE WALTZING MOUSE: You dance honourable waltz?
DOREEN: Ah, go chase yourself, Hirohito. You're not at the Palais now.
J.W.M.: In Japan I am learning to dance since a little mouse. First I learn the Twenty-seven Steps of Perfection, then the Five Heavenly Reverses –
DOREEN: You look a sight in that silly shirt thing.
J.W.M. [*draws sword*]: Do not insult Honourable Waltz Kimono of Royal House!
DOREEN [*languidly, polishing paws*]: Anyway, I seen it in the paper, some scientist, like them psychiatrists on the pitchers, he said if you dance it's because your ears are funny, or something ...

I don't know, though. *Genetics*, although not in the way intended, has once again reminded me that the world is full of marvellous things, which is what all books should do. Carry on, Harmondsworth.

THE SHIP'S DAMP PIPE

One of the most insuperable of literary problems must surely be the composition of directions for emergencies, such as drowning or fire. For there is bound to be a contradiction between the urgency of the crackling building, or the cry from the lake, and the calm, logical paragraphs of small print, numbered like notes on a biology lecture, which are found in parks and office corridors and ship's cabins. Indeed, the only attempt at realistic terseness that I have seen is in the Army notice, to be found in orderly rooms, among the trestle tables and cups of cold tea.

As I remember, this says, in large red letters 'Instructions in case of FIRE. 1 Shout FIRE! 2 Attempt to put it out. 3 Summon assistance. The number of the local Fire Brigade is . . .' It is pleasant to think of the soldier proceeding to some high tower in the barracks and calling out 'FIRE' in a high voice like the muezzin, before 'methodically attempting to put it out'.

Civilian instructions, by contrast, are incurably long-winded. In Hyde Park, for instance, there is by the Serpentine a curious shut-up building, like a small abandoned town hall, with a notice saying 'Royal Life Saving Society'. Near by, there is a notice about drowning and artificial respiration which must run to about 3,000 words. In typography and layout it is similar to those printed sheets dealing with another emergency, The Treatment of Electric Shock, which one always sees in garages. Victim and reviver both have heavy black moustaches and bowler hats.

One feels that if an alarm *was* sounded in Hyde Park

nothing at all would happen for about ten minutes, and then a posse of stalwart, moustachioed men in tight-fitting black costumes, like ballet practice dress, would appear round the corner at a brisk trot, dragging a sort of wooden platform on cartwheels, festooned with big coils of thin rope. An order would be rapped out, and numbers one and two would drop smartly to one knee. ...

The effect of textbook remoteness is greatly heightened when the instructions are in a foreign language. Recently I was reading the German lifejacket direction on the boat to Holland. The *Notsignal*, or Need Signal, is *ein langer Stoss der Schiffsdampfpfeife – one* long blow on the Ship's Damp Pipe. When this signal is given, it says, then shall each Passenger put on a *Schwimveste*, or swim-vest. This is presumably in addition to the life-jacket, which is clearly indicated by another word, *Jacke*. Thus:

Halte die Jacke über den Kopf, stecke die Arme durch die Armlöcher. Sie wird leichter über den Kopf gleiten wenn die hohle Form der Rückseite zuerst gegen den Nacken gehalten und die Vorderseite dann über den Kopf nach unter gezogen wird.

Hold the jacket over the head, stick the arms through the armlocks. You are going to glide it more lightly over the head if the whole form of the rucksack is first held against the neck and the forward side is then yoked over the head from underneath.

It is extraordinarily difficult to visualize these complicated manoeuvres. Can it be that there is a special form of life-jacket in Germany, a huge affair full of straps, like field service marching order, including a rucksack for iron rations, and these armlocks, which the people have been drilled to use from early youth? Possibly this unique apparatus is a relic of German abstention, in Hitler's time, from some Geneva conference about the standardization of lifejackets.

One cannot help feeling that it is an abstention dearly paid for, and bitterly regretted, by the Germans themselves, as they hastily change, down below, into swim-vests, and fumble cursingly with armlocks, and yoke the forward side over the head from underneath, while the cabin tilts and fills with water and the frivolous English and French (there are, strangely enough, no Dutch instructions) leap lightly over the side. Perhaps the Dutch, a practical people full of natural *savoir-faire*, don't need any instructions. Perhaps they just *know*, and are later found calmly waiting to give artificial respiration to these Germans, shivering in their swim-vests and half strangled with sodden canvas. One hopes so.

LABEL BY APPOINTMENT

There is something very mysterious about those cast-iron notice boards with lettering in relief which are found, sometimes round, sometimes diamond-shaped, sometimes oblong, at the ends of decaying lanes by hump-backed canal bridges and obscure level crossings, on tarred fences in abandoned docks, on weedy disused embankments. They belong to an earlier technology than ours, which has now become a subtle, baffling, *indoor* thing, with many little secret grey boxes, transistorized, resisting the amateur screw-driver. They belong to a masculine Victorian spring morning of mechanics; puffs of white steam in a blue sky, the ring of shovels, men in oilskins on windy nights, creaking signals, new cast-iron piers in high tides, tarred planking – the immense solid brand-new Railway itself. Dusty, unread, obscured by tall grass and purple flowers, these notices remember Brunel, even Brindley.

In an age of curious streamlined scrimping – plastic instead of leather, driving-licence holders buff cardboard instead of the good old red cloth (still got mine, boast boast), those new £ notes – they have a lordliness, a lavishness. The people who made them had plenty of time and money to spare, on funny little fusty compartments for Ladies in trains, on complicated park railings, on huge chairs and sideboards with claw feet, on the immense diversification of pubs into many bars separated by scrolled wood and glass, made once only.

The cast-iron notice is the supreme example of this, pushed to the point of paradox; for really it is the *opposite* of printing. Instead of an expensive printing plate containing the letters in reverse, which is then inked and produces many cheap copies (for such was Gutenberg's revolutionary idea), this thing has the letters the right way round; there is only one of it. If you used it for printing everything would come out backwards (except in the case of the word CHIDEOCK. If you print CHIDEOCK on a piece of thin paper which is then held against the light upside-down, it comes out the same, CHIDEOCK. It is a village in Dorset with a population of 800. However).

Even in its first career, industrialism has never been quite so cavalier about economic realities as this, and I have always suspected that these notices came from an older, pre-industrial source. I now claim to have discovered this.

The other evening, walking among the loud silence of reeds where a Suffolk river melts into the sea, I came to a climacteric point, a human statement of concrete and sluices, iron rails and rusty cog-wheels, a reminder on the calm summer evening of the roaring winter floods. Behind me England; lamp-posts, policemen, electric kettles, newsagents, maternity wards, factories. In front of me, vague flats, mud, the sea. Nothing. And there was one of these things. It said, in part, BYE-LAWS ... PROVIDE, INTER ALIA, THAT ANY PERSON INTERFERING WITH OR DAMAGING ANY LAND DRAINAGE WORK, INCLUDING SEA OR RIVER WALLS, SLUICES OR WATERCOURSES ... IS LIABLE ... TO A FINE NOT EXCEEDING £20 AND A FURTHER FINE OF £5 FOR EVERY DAY ON WHICH THE OFFENCE IS COMMITTED OR CONTINUED.

And ah, in the bottom left-hand corner it said, I swear, ROYAL LABEL FACTORY.

This explains everything – the marvellously unpractical, out-of-date wording, the assumption that the kind of people who damage watercourses know what *inter alia* means. At first I saw cloaked figures at night with crowbars (spades? ferrets? gunpowder? How *do* you damage a watercourse?), holding dim lanterns up to read the notice.

'That don't say noathen about *night*, Jem. Lookit, five pun for every day. Hur hur. What be thisyer *inter alia* then? Har, that be Squire's Latin, us can't read un, hur hur.'

But perhaps they *do* know Latin; perhaps damaging sluices is a weird compulsion neurosis that affects overworked scientists. *It's no good, Phoebe, I've struggled against it, but I can't break the sequence, I MUST go down and damage another sluice, this will be the seventh consecutive day....*

But these magic words, ROYAL LABEL FACTORY, I now see, must surely refer to some forgotten sinecure, some aristocratic privilege, some survival like the Pipe of Green Wax or the Elizabethan printing monopolies, that has escaped reform. The Master of the Labels was a job created by Charles II to reward some loyal Royalist; or perhaps it was a job in even earlier times for some royal bastard.

In the Royal Label Factory, hidden away behind Woolwich Arsenal, perhaps, full of antique Caxton presses, there was, as technology advanced, an increasing gap between the actual printing staff and the Master, who would either be a decadent foppish dandy or a red-faced hunting man.

'Cast iron! Damme, what'll you fellers think of next?' such a one might say, on one of his grudging visits to the factory, to the Royal Label Foreman-Sergeant; he would sign the indent without reading it properly, and go back to the Pytcheley. But his son, a weedy scholar, would take an eccentric and embarrassing interest in the proceedings, writing the notices himself, insisting that the letters were not reversed. 'I think they're *b-b-beautiful* things, we m-must p-p-put them up *just* as th-they are....'

It is a pleasant picture. I was quite disappointed, on the only occasion when I have actually telephoned Buckingham Palace and spoken to a Spokesman, to find that it's simply not true.

FORTY GREEN BOTTLES

Four years ago I became a householder (strictly speaking, a mortgagor). By signing incomprehensible documents about curtilage and messuage I crossed the last great gulf between golden, unfettered youth and Responsibility; and within the first three months I thought I knew all there was to know about a man's preoccupation with his house. I learnt that high winds and torrential rain always come at week-ends, when builders have dispersed. Sunday evening is the time for panicky excursions with candles (can't find the torch) into the loft; for agonizing contortions as I try to locate the cracked slate that must surely be causing that spreading patch on the bedroom ceiling.

But of course if one has a light inside the loft one can't expect to see light coming from outside, through a cracked slate, especially as it's dark anyway. I withdraw backwards on my stomach over the dusty beams, my wife guides my descending foot on to the back of the chair she is fearfully holding. Something gives ominously, up there, money falls out of my pockets, I have a crick in my neck. After a night of relentless monsoon and furious wind (what would happen if the house *blew* down, would I still have to go on paying the building society for a non-existent house?) I return at first light on Monday. But no light shows through the roof – and anyway, what could I do if I did find the place? The whole thing is a mad anxious dream, creeping about in the roof while London sleeps.

I have an ear permanently cocked for the pistol-like crack of beams suddenly subsiding with dry rot. I turn off the water at the mere suggestion of a frost; and if there *is* a frost the little grating over the main tap, outside, becomes frozen over in the night; I go into the shed, in my dressing-gown, to find the chisel to lever it open, I grope in the grey light, and hundreds of tins fall down with what the Elizabethans described as *heyho rumbelo*.

But there is something more than this. After these four years I have discovered that this preoccupation with the mere fabric of the house is only the beginning. The householder is concerned not only with this death force, with the huge, hydra-headed forces of seediness and decay, but also, for much more of his time, with a strange, perverted life-force as well. For the fact is that a house actually *generates small heavy objects*. The householder must conceive of his house as though it were a jar containing a colourless, impalpable liquid, the ground of life, in which are suspended many non-soluble objects which tend to sink to the bottom. The higher the specific gravity of the things, naturally, the quicker they sink. It is not a matter of size. It is quite natural for a bed – big, soft, fairly light – to stay upstairs. It is the small, dense objects which form a sediment at the bottom of the house unless one keeps everything in constant agitation.

In the bottoms of cupboards, in the lower part of the house, a heavy, concentrated sediment is constantly forming; of dense piles of damp magazines, old vacuum flasks with mouldy corks, heavy little gramophone motors, ice skates, gas rings, headlamps, a secondhand-looking pile of about *thirty* dinner plates with those gold edges. And, of course, bottles. We put as many in the dustbin as we dare, and heaven knows what orgies the dustmen think go on in our house. But the bottom of our house is inexorably filling up with bottles.

We possess an extremely heavy little Oriental table, a charming wedding present which, nevertheless, doesn't belong, somehow, in our small drawing-room. We keep it in the spare bedroom. But it keeps coming downstairs. Periodically we find ourselves panting and grunting round narrow angles of the stairs, taking it up again. It is made of some dense Oriental wood, full of sharp corners that tear the wallpaper. I don't remember ever bringing it downstairs (which would be just as awkward, and therefore just as memorable). But we have carried it up at least four times.

We bought our shed, as we innocently thought, to house the pram and garden tools. But now the pram will hardly go in; to get at the shears I must remove vast bundles of heavy carpet, things keep sliding down – a strange bath made of papiermâché, big old attaché cases that seem to be full of tinsel and curtains, a tremendous spindly easel inextricably locked with a bucket, miles of rope – and of course more bottles.

And then there are the boots and shoes. The other day, on a long car journey, we turned off the main road, deep into the silent country, for a picnic lunch. We stopped in a tiny lane. Cows lowed, birds sang, leaves rustled. There was a gentle, earthy smell; no houses were in sight. I walked ten yards from the car, and there, in a ditch, lay at least two hundred old shoes. There were bits of charred paper; some-one had made half-hearted attempts to burn them. Some householder had driven out all this way, the back of his small car crammed with shoes, shoes spilling forward over the front seats whenever he braked. . . .

Before I became a householder I should have dismissed this strange, ugly pile as mere urban vandalism. But now it's given me an idea.

THE LOSS FORCE

One of the mysterious ways in which the material world reminds us that we do not control it is by abstracting personal possessions from us. In our brash human way we then say that *we* have lost them; but in fact we have not done anything, we have been acted on by the Loss Force. This is analogous to, and much more mysterious than, Shaw's Life Force.

Who has not known that feeling, almost of terror, when one searches a room for a book that one saw five minutes ago? Yes, it was on that table, in the cosy, intellectually ordered world in which we were living before we missed it. But after this awful, this magical disappearance, we resort to methods of discovery which mere intellect tells us are mad.

We look under large articles of furniture that have not been moved for months. We telephone our friends and ask if they've borrowed it. We look in the bathroom, under the bed, more and more wildly. These are not rational acts; they are a kind of possessed ritual, to propitiate the Loss Force.

On a select band of us the Loss Force acts in a special manner, just as a kind of racial wisdom and innocence operates through the type of Dostoyevsky's Idiot. People like me are dedicated to it. I lose pens and matches and glasses and handkerchiefs all the time; and every four months or so there is a Grand Loss – a spare wheel, an overcoat, a typewriter (if that was only burglars, why didn't they take anything *else*?).

I have been able to organize my life on a rather beautiful, resigned acceptance of these facts. But it is a resignation that has only recently healed the scars made, three or four years ago, by the dreadful fear that I had been selected by the Loss Force *to lose other people's things as well.*

My friend Harblow, who had stayed on in the Army, was passing through London, and I put him up on a Friday night. He had business in South London on Saturday morning. I was working in Baker Street. We arranged to meet for lunch; and to save him carting his bag around I was to take it to the office and hand it over at the restaurant.

I got on the bus with his bag. Near Marble Arch I saw the bus I wanted for Baker Street coming down Park Lane. I leapt lightly off the first bus and on to the second. We had gone about 300 yards, to Portman Square, when I remembered Harblow's bag. For once this wasn't a crawler bus, but I got off it somehow. I hailed the first taxi that came – an incredibly old one, driven by a man like a walrus. Indeed, he seemed to be some sort of manifestation of the Loss Force. I could feel it in the air throughout that ghastly day, informing the cold grey buildings, making London hostile, brooding, and unhelpful.

It seemed ludicrous to be chasing anything, even a bus, in this high, pram-like machine. Nevertheless, I breathlessly instructed the dotard to drive furiously down Wigmore Street, which is parallel to Oxford Street, and try to intercept the bus at Oxford Circus. We lumbered off. All the lights were against us. We got stuck in an appalling jam. No bus.

I telephoned London Transport and asked them what was the earliest hour at which a 12, a 17, or an 88 (for it could have been any of these) could be coming back again. They didn't seem at all taken aback by this appalling poser. I heard a rustle of pages, then a voice said, 11.31. So at 11.30 I stood outside the C. & A. For two hours I stood at the head of the queue, looking in every bus, in the little place under the stairs, but never getting in. It must have looked mad. No bag.

I had a sad lunch with Harblow. The bag, he said, contained his service dress, his squash racket and clothes, his camera, pyjamas and shaving tackle, £15, all the papers for a court-martial in which he was the prosecuting officer on the following Monday. I saw the headlines, OFFICER GAVE FRIEND SECRET PAPERS, COURT TOLD. OFFICER HELD ON BUS BAG LOSS. MR X TELLS COURT PSYCHIATRIST OF 'LOSS FORCE'....

That afternoon I found out enough about London Transport's layout and running schedules to write a script for a training film. I made calls to countless garages. 'Just a minute,' a voice would say; and for a quarter of an hour I would hear hollow echoing bangs, and whistling, and engines, and cinema organ music; then the voice would say, 'No, I'm sorry' . . . And all the time the crooks were photostating the court-martial papers, sharing out the £15, taking the camera to a 'fence'. Or were they? Had the bag, in fact, just *disappeared*?

But at six o'clock the Loss Force realized it had got the wrong man. The bag was in a garage at Merton. Now if it had been *mine* . . .

HARLEY STREET

I have always thought that if I were a British Council Official showing some Eastern potentate, like the Akhond of Swat or the Zigzag of Gong, round London, I should make him feel at home straight away by pointing out the capital's curious habit of grouping trades together in streets, as they do in Eastern bazaars.

'This is Fleet Street, the Street of Scribes,' I should say, 'and here is Savile Row, the Street of Tailors,' Then there would be Lombard Street, the Street of Money Changers; Hatton Garden, the Street of Diamonds; Chancery Lane, the Street of Lawyers; Warren Street, the Street of Automobile Dealers. And, of course, there would be Harley Street, the Street of Doctors.

Of course, the Zigzag would be disappointed if he expected to find a roaring, colourful thoroughfare, with doctors sitting cross-legged in open booths and shouting to passers-by 'Sir! I got lovely appendix knife. I cut you up, very cheap, very good.' For Harley Street is nothing if not dignified and quiet. I used to live in a mews at the back of Harley Street, and I was almost the only person in the whole square mile who didn't have a Rolls-Royce.

I bet there's a bigger concentration of Rolls-Royces in Harley Street than anywhere else in the world. There are old, high Rolls-Royces, with solemn, deep horns like the *Queen Mary*'s siren. There are shiny, new Rolls-Royces, some painted over with that extraordinary pattern to look like wickerwork. And for the younger, more dashing specialists, there are the nearest that Rolls-Royces ever came to sporting

models – those old tourers. As a matter of fact, I'm not at
all sure they're all real Rolls-Royces, with engines. I suspect
that some of them are just plywood models, with nothing
at all inside. They just stand all day for show, and are
towed away by horses late at night.

It's a wonder to me how all these Rolls-Royces remain in
such good condition, because the Harley Street area is one
of the two most dangerous for driving in London. The other
is Soho. Both these districts were laid out in the precise,
mathematical manner of the Georgians, and both are therefore full of busy right-angle crossings with the views blocked
by tall corner buildings.

If you stand around long enough in Soho you are bound
to see, from a good vantage point, a taxi and a car converging.
You say to yourself 'That taxi's going to hit that car', and
it *does*. It's a wonderful, godlike feeling; but it's even better
around Harley Street, because the chances are it'll be two
Rolls-Royces.

But more fascinating even than Rolls-Royce crashes, to the
casual bystander in this area, are the shops. I first noticed
them long before I lived anywhere near. I noticed them when
I started going to the Wigmore Hall. This, naturally enough,
is in Wigmore Street, which forms one boundary of the
Doctors' District. All concerts at the Wigmore Hall end at
five minutes past nine, a horribly empty hour when it's too
early to go home and too late to start anything else.

It is always raining when you come out into Wigmore
Street, that is not quite in the West End; and you drift about
aimlessly, wondering what to do next, when you find youself
looking at these terrible shops they have for doctors. Apart
from fairly harmless things, like doctors' bags and those cold
horsehair couches they all have, these shops sell awful
things like bent nut-crackers, all chromium-plated and
gleaming.

There are chromium-plated saws, and frightful tweezers
and spikes and needles, and things like toast-racks with
knurled screws, for holding the body open while they get on
with whatever they're doing. There are dreadful extending

tubes, like the legs of camera tripods only with *knives* and lights at the end. There are even chromium-plated hammers. There are complicated machines for giving anaesthetics, complete with chromium-plated spanners; and lewd, bulging things made of red rubber.

Some shops crowd their windows with these horrors. Others just have a table-cloth laid out with one chromium-plated mincer lying tastefully on it, like the one hat in a Bond Street milliner's. And there is one shop where they have all these things only *four times as big*, for veterinary surgeons.

It was only when I saw all this stuff, some of which is made on the premises, that I began to realize that this is a district of craftsmen, too, to realize that there are people who spend their whole lives making these de-luxe tools. The other day I saw a letter in a magazine called *Packaging*, a very tasteful publication, which is usually full of bright suggestions for cornflake packets or toothpaste caps so ingenious that the public will be practically forced to buy whatever brand adopts them. This letter was headed:

CONTAINERS FOR HUMAN ORGANS

Sir,

We are suppliers of every type of equipment for hospitals and other public bodies and institutions, and are at present seeking alternatives to the 5 in. by $7\frac{1}{2}$ in. diameter waxed containers, which we cannot now obtain.

These are required to hold human organs for short periods, must of course be completely watertight and have a tight-fitting lid, and be of approximately the capacity indicated by the measurements quoted above. Any suggestions you can make will be greatly appreciated by ourselves and by hospital authorities throughout the country.

Why five inches by seven and a half inches? You couldn't get a human leg in a container that size. But I bet you could get them all sizes in those shops around Harley Street. I bet you could get them five by seven and a half feet. I bet you could get *anything* in those shops.

In the artistes' room at the Wigmore Hall, among the signed photographs of Kreisler and Paderewski, there is a picture of a man in sober Edwardian clothes standing beside what looks like an enormous Meccano model, in the middle of which is what looks like a violin. In fact it *is* a violin, and this is a machine for playing it, a violin version of the pianola.

Well, I wouldn't mind betting that this contraption started life in some workshop at the back of Harley Street, as a help to some devilish operation. And then after a few people had died the man changed it into a violin-playing machine – cat guts instead of people's. They're clever, those people in Harley Street.

A DIVERSITY OF DOCTORS

Every layman, in his heart, has the same feeling about doctors that Dr Johnson had about soldiers and sailors – a vague sense of inferiority. Indeed this sense is not even vague, but very specific, when the doctor is actually lifting the layman's eyelid, saying *H'm* in a rather frightening way, or just listening to his stethoscope. How meaningless the sounds in this instrument would be to the layman! If he has any ideas at all in his frivolous, unmedical head, he imagines, perhaps, that a healthy man would make a sort of amplified roaring and bumping, something like this: GLUP, *hoo-oogh haa-aagh*, GLUP – the *Glup* being the heartbeat and *hoo-oogh haa-aagh* being the breath. And perhaps in a man with bronchitis, GLUP *hoo-oogh* – *achicka-snurk-hoo-aagh* GLUP *achicka-snurk.* . . .

But these and all such guesses remain unanswered; he would never dare to ask. That sort of thing is elementary to the doctor, who learnt all about râles and rhonchi years ago, poring over his books in some monastic little room while the layman was taking out golden girls, drinking, smoking, eating, reading novels – and look at him now, not at all sure which side of his body his liver is, or what it does.

Medical knowledge is the only kind of knowledge that is indisputably both true and good. To the layman, scientists as a whole are rather sinister figures in white coats, as likely as not making bombs. Philosophers spend years at universities, and all we get out of it is some voice on the Third Programme saying, for instance, 'These propositions may thus be reduced to three. *A is A*; *some A is A*; and *A is not*

A.' Lawyers are even more doubtful; they blind you with statements like '... assigns unto the Mortgagees first ALL AND SINGULAR the freehold premises first hereby mortgaged or any part thereof and determines any such tenancy' (any tenancy such as what?) – and they always leave you with £150 less than you thought you'd have.

But doctors, ah, that's a different matter. Some people disguise their feelings by acting aggressive, like Shaw, who roundly asserted that 'religious belief has certainly not died out in England. It has merely been transferred to the General Medical Council'; or like the persons one always meets in hospital, who talk of heroic arguments they had with doctors *and won*; 'so he told me he was going to do a lobectomy, and of course I wasn't having *that*'. But most of us wouldn't dare.

So overpowering is this feeling that doctors are different from laymen that it is with a shock that one realizes that doctors are different from each other, too. The layman gets his first inkling of this when, some time in his twenties, he suddenly realizes that there are Old Doctors and Young Doctors. Until then, all doctors had seemed the same – bald, bespectacled, rather severe men, with hard, cold fingers. It is not very long before the layman realizes, with a start, that not only are there Young Doctors, there are some *younger than himself*. It is a fearful milestone in life when not only policemen but doctors begin to seem young. And it is at this point that the layman starts to classify them. He will never be as good as a doctor, but he simply can't go on with this crude father-figure of his school-days. Doctors are men like himself, only better, and he must work out some scheme for fitting them into the general experience of life. And what a rich, various classification it is! For example:

THE SCHOOL DOCTOR

As above, bald, bespectacled, etc. Aged about 50, always has been, always will be. Has difficulty focusing his eyes on you, always talks over your body to Matron, or the Headmaster, or, if no one else in room, to invisible third person. Lives in a black saloon car, from which he appears every Tuesday morning. Grunts or hums to himself. Is last experienced – not alone but *en masse* – at call-up medical board. He is then exchanged for

THE ARMY DOCTOR

Reaches nadir of impersonality and mystery and *untouchability*, after army doctor the tide begins to turn. When you are a private he is godlike, aloof, forever inoculating you and suspecting you of having abominable diseases. If he has any communication to make to you it is by way of a rather nasty corporal. When, or if, you are commissioned you make bluff jokes in the mess and call him Doc; he is always taking one of your 15–cwts.

THE FRIEND DOCTOR

Husband of girl you know. Very gay, tells wonderful stories of legendary figures at teaching hospital (e.g. Famous crusty specialist, seeing outpatients for post-operative treatment, does not recognize one woman. She says 'Well, sir, it's me 'usband; 'e's a cobbler and got a lot of work in just now, so 'e couldn't come. 'E says all you do is just test 'is water, so 'e asked me to bring this bottle for 'im.' 'He did, eh?' grunts specialist. 'Nurse, give me another bottle.' Goes behind screen, sound of bottle being filled. Emerges. 'Here's a sample of my water, take it home to your husband and tell him to make me a pair of shoes'). Friend doctor has Early Struggles, goes away to live in some remote hospital for year. Has old car, smokes pipe, likes Bach, plays flute, likes Goon Show. Splendid. But really gives you false sense of knowing doctors, what goes on behind mask.

THE INSURANCE DOCTOR

Works in a curious place half consulting-room, half-office, with carpet and glass-fronted bookcases, lots of shiny wood.

Asks about your grandparents, taps you with hammers, fills in huge forms. Seems abstracted. Surrounded by photographs, handsome women with pearls, mountains, trout rivers, hints of rather leisurely, beautiful life, rose garden in Surrey, sons at University. Probably neighbours don't even know he is a doctor.

BEAT-YOU-AT-OWN-GAME DOCTOR

If you are literary gent, this doctor, as well as being very good doctor, has read whole of Proust. In French. Knows about Auden, Rilke, Kierkegaard. If you play golf, he has lots of cups, won years ago (and is probably Scots, they're *all* brilliant). If you are musician, he knows opus numbers of all Beethoven quartets, Koechel numbers of Mozart, is good pianist. None of these talents flaunted, indeed it has to be dragged out of him. But clearly could have succeeded in many other walks of life as well as that of doctor.

HOSPITAL DOCTOR

(*a*) *Junior*. Dedicated. Tremendous quiet charm. Face has good bones. Answers silly questions reasonably. Nice to nurses.

(*b*) Senior. Nasty to nurses. Goes round like bishop in procession, headed by acolytes. Parries all questions. Makes jokes.

SPECIALIST

Extraordinary impression of *space*. If you go to see him he is in a cool room twenty feet high, nothing in it but desk, vast carpet, horsehair couch, small gas fire. No equipment, all that sort of thing used by ordinary doctors; he just *thinks*. If he comes to see you (or your wife) your house suddenly seems small, he has to duck at doors, his car is too big to be parked anywhere near you, you feel apologetic he had to walk. (There don't seem to be any small specialists. Presumably there are, little round jolly Welsh ones, but you never seem to meet them.) Addresses you by surname.

FOREIGN DOCTOR

When you get ill in Spain, Switzerland, France, anywhere abroad. Has incised black marble slab at entrance to huge apartment block, all stone floors and wrought-iron gates. He lives on third floor. Three small pale children giggle and whisper in foreign language in next room, you seem to be waiting in drawing-room. He has two gold teeth, tells you he has been to London. Invariably prescribes penicillin.

*

The foregoing may not be exact reflections of reality. But they are closer to it than the conventional doctors of fiction such as

THE WOMAN'S MAGAZINE DOCTOR

Called Nigel or Stephen. Strong chin, blue eyes. Simple about women. Is attracted by flirtatious lady visitor to hospital Open Day (Paula, Vanessa) who has cream sports car, never notices nurse heroine (Jill, Valerie) till she is very efficient in some crisis (fire, accident, or, in tropics, cholera).

AMERICAN FILM DOCTOR

(a) *Young*. Wears a sort of miner's headlamp all the time. Gets mixed up with crooks to clear someone's name. Takes bullet out of gangster while other gangster watches behind curtain with gun.

(b) *Old*. Drinks. Tries to forget. Look at these hands. Surgeon's hands. Yeah. Crisis in lonely farmhouse, woman having baby. You got to help. No, I can't do it. Sock on jaw. I guess I deserved that. Right. I shall want lots of hot water. Tense, sweat. Thunderstorm, torrential Hollywood rain.

Waa-aah, infant cries, wan smile from mother. Gonna be all right. Dawn.

*

And before we finish, let us not forget

THE WOMAN DOCTOR

Like a sort of sober comet, swims into and out of your life. When you are in hospital, she has two patients in your ward. They think she is marvellous. Always wears white coat. A friend of your aunt's goes to one, says she is marvellous. She is invariably married, to another doctor (do they get party invitations saying 'Dr and Dr' instead of 'Dr and Mrs'?); he thinks she is marvellous. Well, she *is* marvellous. All doctors are marvellous.

INK AND GOO

Remove the protective piepe below by turning the knop to the left the piston perceptible in the tube is screwed down. Dip the sylo-pen in the ink about 2 cm. By slowly turning to the right, the piston is screwed up again until it cracks ...

Eventual trouble in using the stylo-pen with regard to the flowing in of ink goo back to the stopping of the writing pipe with filaments of paper, dust, or incrusted ink ...

Take notice that the srewing in is donne by holding the fountain pen upright very carefully, or otherwise the thin wire will be bent and squeezad
– Instructions with German PISTON FOUNTAIN PEN

> Fountain pens, vain useless baubles,
> Fill the writer's life with traubles
> Yet I'm fiddling once again
> With silly piston fountain pen
> Hoping, this time, skill Teutonic
> Has o'ercome those defects chronic
> (Nib bone-dry when pen just filled,
> When near-empty, blobs all spilled):
> See, I'll follow this directive,
> First removing piepe protective;
> That must be this thing here – stop!
> Have I turned too far the knop?
> Surely vacuum will be lacking
> If I screw up till it's cracking?
> If I have correctly donne
> Now the ink should sweetly ronne.
> Perceptible in tube, the piston
> Should fill up a sac-like cistern,
> But careful, upright though its poise is

INK AND GOO

All I get is sucking noises,
Ink is on my fingers too –
Not just ink, but ink and goo,
Writing pipe with goo incrusted,
Squeezad wire all bent and busted;
Even German pens won't write
But fill with goo and *Schrecklichkeit**
Leading me a merry caper
With goo and filaments and paper.
O vile! O sylo! I'll omit
Such engines from my writing kit
And like man of commonsense 'll
Use the good old HB pencil.

*Frightfulness

133

THE MICE WILL PLAY

Of course, one reason why the whole idea of Japanese waltzing mice is so fascinating is that we are faintly surprised and pleased to detect, however fancifully, a human note so far down in the scheme of creation. There is a vast dark penumbra of idiot or hostile things that we can never know – amoebae, crabs, newts – and flies, forever buzzing about, alighting, and neurotically rubbing their hands like Lady Macbeth. But the moment we get into the mammal class here are these little creatures, with their beady, knowing eyes, capering away down there in tiny mirth, and 'Good gracious', we say: 'it's just like a waltz.' We are in our own part of the spectrum. We do not have to wait until we get to the intelligent primates, to the Chimpanzees' Tea Party, before we see something we think we recognize.

Mice are the point at which the Hegelian Idea, the world becoming self-conscious, really gets going. It is significant that in Beatrix Potter the smallest characters, beneath which life is obviously not intelligible, are Mr John Dormouse and Timmie Willie. There is no smaller (or more basic) cartoon figure than Mickey Mouse. Indeed, if we imagine a sort of reverse process of creation, analogous to that of running tape backwards through a tape recorder, so that human beings came out all garbled, small, jerky, madly nimble and high-pitched, but still vestigially recognizable, we can see *ourselves* as mice.

I once played the harmonium at a wedding, and on one of the bellows there was affixed a stamped metal plate saying:

MOUSE-PROOF PEDAL

This seems to express perfectly our curious, ambivalent relationship with mice. It somehow seems both natural and extraordinary at the same time. It is natural because *all* types of mouse would seem at home in a harmonium. We can picture church mice living there quietly, in a dim light filtering through the green cloth at the back. But we can also imagine the gayer, more theatrical type of mouse, perhaps even the Japanese waltzer, taking naturally to it. For despite its ecclesiastical veneer, there is something showy about a harmonium. To play it requires the same sort of skill as that of a music-hall juggler; it is a kind of holy one-man band.

In playing the harmonium no part of the body is unoccupied. One pedals with one's feet, and sometimes there is a knob called *Prolongement*, operated with one's heel, as well. With the knees one moves wooden flaps that control the volume. With the hands, of course, one both plays and works the stops. If one pulls the wrong one, everything below middle C suddenly drops about four octaves; the church is filled with a gruff, reedy bumbling, well described by the stop-name *Bourdon*.

There is a wanton, nineteenth-century air about the whole thing. The harmonium was preceeded by exotic inventions, with names such as Organo-Violine, Aerophone, Aeolophone, Seraphine. All kinds of sensual and voluptuous effects were devised by bearded Frenchmen. Stops are called *Voix Celeste*, or simply *Expression*, and there is a tremendous roaring one called *Grand Jeu*. It is easy to imagine not only Japanese Waltzing Mice, but French Cancan Mice, scandalizing their church brethren with tiny bacchanalian squeaks as the *Grand Jeu* brings some wild dance to its climax.

And yet it *is* extraordinary too. Doubtless a harmonium, with its rods and pallets, its wires and struts, its tubes and passages, its little doors opening and shutting, might at first seem like an exciting playground specially made for mice, a delicious three-dimensional maze, with comfortable leather bellows to sleep on after the merry games were over; but surely the first experience of the thing being played would be so traumatic as to scare them off for ever. It would suddenly go all dark, there would be a monstrous gale of wind, terrible clankings and creakings would strike terror into the heart of the stoutest mouse; trap-doors would open, floors would tilt, and then an unbelievable, an unbearable intensity of sound would compass them about. Surely any mice that escaped would tell their fellows that this enormous palace was in reality just a new and diabolical form of mouse-trap, designed to *kill with sound.* . . .

But there it is. Obviously mice have got into harmonia in sufficient numbers to make this special pedal necessary. How were they discovered? Can it really be that someone, playing *Evening Meditation* or *Simple Voluntary*, noticed another, a shriller note, a tiny squeaking, above the throbbing *Voix Celeste*? Or, finding the bellows lacking in power for the *Grand Jeu*, discovered the tell-tale teeth marks in the leather? And how do they *test* the Mouse-Proof Pedal? 'O.K., Mr Bates, the action's fine. Let's just try it for mice.' . . .

I should like to think they have a special test piece called *Three Deaf Mice.*

THE BIRDS

In the modern city, an abstract certainty of building and buses imposed on the wild earth, there are only two phenomena that cut across the dry human mechanics, the endless organization of street and stone, and remind us of the waiting jungle. These are the weather and the birds. No building is too tall to shut out the casual magnificence of cloudscapes, no street immune from the Pentecostal wind; the birds are blithely uncontrolled. Singly they fly, or, blown against the green evening sky like a huge twisting mat, the starlings make a gesture over our temples. For a lost second their twittering is a communication; we remember the Roman augurs, the fortunes of the State depending on the flight of birds.

Birds, in fact, are symbolic. They come with irrational magic from strange lands, from empty northern spaces or the musky south; and it is simply no good to treat them merely as a public nuisance in towns. There is a curious air of unreality about all these official attempts to get rid of starlings. In Birmingham, *The Times* reported recently:

A 'boosted' recording of the cries of an alarmed hen starling is directed at the roosts high up on the buildings. When it is playing at full volume the birds take off, echoing the alarm notes. Although they return, experts believe that the recording will leave a lasting impression and that ultimately the birds will move to another district – 'which is', as one official said, 'as much as we can hope for'.

In spite of the boosted recording, all this seems not so much scientific as *ritual*. High up on the windy pediment of some such building as Birmingham Town Hall is this delegation, composed of gramophone technicians, journalists, and aldermen in red robes. Up in the grey air, they clutch at the legs of Victorian goddesses of plenty and industry, they steady themselves against classical grapes and spears. Far below, ant-like figures move in and out of university and art gallery; the life of the city goes on, watched over by municipal statues in toga or top hat. An alderman gives a solemn sign. The monstrously magnified cry of the alarmed hen fills the upper air, intolerable screeching echoes roll down among the streets and are blown, by the buffeting Midland wind, back at the tiny figures up on the ledge. Birmingham has spoken to the birds.

The same thing goes on in Trafalgar Square and elsewhere. And always there is this impression that the ultimate object is not to get rid of the birds but to make a gesture. When the civic party is panting up the narrow ladders, laden with accumulators, amplifiers, and heavy civic emblems – maces, antlers, old magic horns perhaps – no one in his heart really wants the birds to go away. On the way down, some official says, 'Well, I bet that left a lasting impression.' Everybody else nods, but they know what he means really. They are all perfectly sure it hasn't had the slightest effect.

Indeed, it would be quite embarrassing if the birds did 'move to another district' (one imagines them packing their nests, like people packing furniture). It wouldn't help matters if the telephone rang half an hour later in the Town Hall and a voice said crossly, 'This is Wolverhampton. Look here, we've got all these damn starlings of yours. They seem scared out of their wits. Can't hear ourselves speak in the Civic Centre.'

No, there is a sort of purposeful pointlessness about the whole thing. Anybody who really wanted to get rid of starlings could think of half a dozen methods more practical than the ones we read about. Long trays of special liquid glue could be placed on the public roofs. Sacks of poisoned breadcrumbs would be a perfectly simple way. But instead of this, the starlings are the excuse for wonderfully obscure experiments which everyone knows will not work. One has only to think of this record of the alarmed hen starling being made. How was it done? Was a microphone concealed in the cage of some lonely bird while someone made frightful faces at it, or showed it his cat?

It is all of a piece with the other methods reported – the ultrasonic frequencies, the divinely mysterious rays. We may expect other equally fantastic attempts. Huge blowing machines will be set up, establishing monstrous mechanical hurricanes against which no bird could land. Aerial trawls will be lowered from helicopters. And so on. Whatever method is used, it will be perfectly harmless, so that, behind the splendid panoply of urban organization, we may properly make this statement that we have to do with the birds, and they with us.

PLAY ON

It cannot be an accident that traditional representations of heaven give pride of place to music. Those angels, with their delicate strong Italian faces, in their bright local paradise, make a consort of sweet sounds with the flageolet and the *tromba marina* or *Nonnengeige*,* with the shagbut and the Dudelsack, the trumpet and the triangle – arp, arp, ting ting, deedle eedle ee; or their lips are parted in soundless song. Yet we know that these tiny tunes, these man-size madrigals, are mere figures and allegories for the tremendous music of the spheres, for the mountains that skip like rams, for the huge harmony of the stars; for a singing, celestial order at once rushing and still.

The angels are never depicted as painting, or as carving statues, or as painfully scratching out verses. No, it is by means of music, so abstract in its pure relations, yet so real, that they relate the One to the many. As Schubert said, it is the divine art.

But even on this earth music has an enormous advantage over the other arts, in that we are physically present at the miracle, we see the musicians while the fire and the light are actually upon them. It is true we do not see the composer at work, any more than we do the painter or the poet. But we do see the musicians. Among the music-stands, there lie the lovely symbolic shapes of instruments – the shining horn curled about its entrails, that can send forth a basic, visceral cry from the world's heart or can chuckle with divine joy (in

---

* Because it is, or was, played by nuns. It is a kind of one-stringed fiddle.

a Mozart horn concerto); the guardee trombones, the womby cellos. And when the musicians come into the hall, and take up their instruments, and assume the physical positions for making their marvellous precise din, there is an integrity, a holiness about them. No matter how plain they may be in themselves, once the rapt tenseness of execution is upon them, there is a touch, however distant, of that expression of the angels; a withdrawal in the eyes, something in the line of the mouth.

It is this 'holiness' that enables music, when combined with other arts and techniques, to triumph over the muddy imperfections implicit in their grosser origins. At an opera we go right on enjoying the glorious sound even while the chorus, one eye anxiously on the conductor, exaggeratedly hails a jerkily moving cardboard ship, or drinks from ludicrous wooden goblets, when pages bring candelabra that snap on with 4-volt precision, when the doors of prison cells keep being pulled to by a shirt-sleeved hand. The pitfalls of language, because of all-flowing music, do not worry us. I remember being transported, at a concert given by Elisabeth Schumann, even while my eye ran down the programme and fell on a song called *Mausfallensprüchlein*, and the absurd but ineradicable idea leapt into my mind that this means 'The Little Speech of a Fallen Mouse'.

It is this 'holiness', too, that makes the presence of hired musicians at a non-musical function, such as a dinner, so oddly embarrassing. We are uneasily aware, through the merry conversations and the clatter of plates, that a vestigial glory, a kind of tarnished god, is among us. What goes on behind that violinist's face, as he ploughs through the routine of *Waldteufeliana*? Does he despise us all? Is he thinking only of the music? We cannot believe that he is simply thinking of his fee. This embarrassment causes some to talk louder, to ignore the music. With me it takes the form of clapping loudly.

Once I was in the restaurant of a large Mediterranean hotel. It was the peak hour of nine o'clock; businessmen in those tropical gaberdine suits, with their families, American naval officers, a chattering cosmopolitan crowd kept the waiters busy. Corks popped under the palms, exotic sweets were concocted in the silent *woof* of spirit-stove explosions. And in one corner four musicians were playing, of all things, a Mozart quartet. Utterly unheeded, as they probably were originally by the Prince-Bishop of Salzburg's guests, the perfect phrases created their universe again.

It was good playing, and at the end I clapped. For a second there was complete silence, heads turned towards me in surprise; there were a few half-hearted echoes, then the hubbub began again. The violinist gave me a low smiling bow. Then the woman pianist pulled his sleeve and showed him some music. He smiled again; and for me, the Englishman, they played a funny, thin little arrangement of *Greensleeves*. I'm sure *they* weren't just thinking of the fee.

SLEEP FOR SALE

I write this article with a certain reluctance, because it is going to enable someone to make a fortune that I could make myself if I had £10,000 capital. For, extraordinary though it may seem, there is in London and other great cities a potential demand for a commodity that no one, up till now, has ever thought of supplying – *sleep*.

I mean of course sleep in the daytime. It is all very well to say that the man who is tired of London is tired of life. There are times – after one of those jolly lunches that end at half past three, after exhausting shuffling about in shops, or perhaps simply after a long train journey that has brought one too early for one's appointment – when all the glories of the capital seem as dust. Perhaps if we actually made the effort, say, to go and see Constable's *Cornfield* in the National Gallery, once we were there we should walk into the painter's rustling summer vision, all tiredness forgotten. Perhaps some matinée is beginning of a play that would change our lives. Perhaps, in some white and gold hall, Mozart is being played that would lift us out of the body into the third heaven. But at half past three all this seems unlikely. All we really want to do is to lie down for an hour.

But where? It would be ridiculous to hire a hotel room just for an hour's rest. There are only about three days a year when it's dry and warm enough in the Park. We end up by going into a news theatre (and coming out with a headache) or sitting over an unwanted cup of nasty coffee and a tomato sandwich (4s. 3d.).

Now it is not enough just to sell sleep. It must be, as it were, packaged, everything must be done in a modern, streamlined manner. (Milk, for instance, just as ancient and pre-industrial as sleep, is sold from an irresistible machine, just outside the *Observer* office: you put 6d. in, there is a lot of clunking and thumping inside, then a tremendously modern triangular cardboard thing comes out, full of milk.) The first thing to do is to have a good trade name, and I have already thought of this: ZIZ-O-MATIC.

With my £10,000 I should open the first of a chain of ZIZ-O-MATICS. I should rent some premises in the Tired Square Mile, and fit it out with little booths, about ten feet by six, painted in restful colours and containing simply a single bed and a giant version of those towel machines – a blanket machine (BLANKETMASTER, Reg'd). Two florins in the mechanism of the door would start a time-clock. At the end of an hour a melodious chime would ring out, and three minutes after that the bed would gently tip over (unless of course you had put in four florins, for two hours). Sixpence in the BLANKETMASTER (Reg'd) would cause it to emit an adequate length of clean, sterilized blanket.

There would naturally be complete segregation and complete respectability – one floor for ladies and one for gentlemen. Apart from cleaners, each floor would require a staff of just one: an elderly but physically strong person of the appropriate sex who would control admission and occasionally look through the little spyhole in the door of every booth to see that all was well.

I don't see how it could fail. In a floor space of merely 60 ft by 30 I could get twenty booths, giving me forty on my two floors. That's £8 an hour, and even if I were full only for Peak Tiredness Time (2 p.m.–5 p.m.) that's £24 a day, £168 a week, £8,736 a year.

These are minimum figures. I am certain that at any given time there are hundreds of people in central London who would cheerfully pay 4s. 6d. for an hour's sleep. As a responsible businessman, however, I should make my first ZIZ-O-MATIC modest and experimental: even if I found that people considered 4s. 6d. too steep I could halve the charge and still make £4,368 a year.

But I am sure the thing would develop. There would be a few *de luxe* booths with proper sheets, etc., for those who wished to undress for their rest (6s. an hour, I think). The original ancillary services (washing and toilet facilities) would be extended; there would be gay little snack bars and lounges. 'Meet you at the ZIZ-O-MATIC' would become a popular phrase, the lounges would be the cheerfullest places in London. Well supplied with playbills, running their own ticket agencies, they would be full of laughing, zestful people, restored, full of vitality, agog to plunge once more into the infinite, never-ending life of London.

Over to you, capitalists. But, remember, I thought of it first.

A DREAM OF BUILDERS

When all that debate about the 300,000 houses was going on it was curious how everyone spoke as if building were just another industry, as if the problem were simply one of co-ordinating timber stocks. Anyone who has ever watched builders at work, studying the formal, slow decency of their movements, knows that they are ritualists. They perform a solemn, magic dance, as a result of which their curious heaps of *old* things, rusty pipes and planks and derelict-looking, upside-down baths, are miraculously transformed into new houses. It's no good telling proper English builders that a house is a *machine à habiter*, or prating of prefabrication. They know better. Chesterton described a staircase as a railway to the moon; now there was a man who understood why builders are dreamy.

Lately I have been able to study builders at work in a place where even the most unimaginative passer-by is reminded that building is a necromancy, a stone dream which might be blown away at any moment; for I now live opposite a bombed site.

Across the wild-flowered cellar there has been built a thing described on a prohibitory notice to the public as 'this gantry'. It is a bridge made of scaffolding; and there are always men on this bridge, at any time of the day (rather as there is always one old engine, going backwards, on that railway bridge at the bottom of Fleet Street).

Sometimes the men have wheel-barrows, sometimes they walk alone; but it is always with a rapt, unhurried mien. If two of them meet there is always a short, formal greeting, then one man turns back with his new companion. If there were only a boat and a woman the thing would be a permanent modern tableau of the Willow Pattern. One has a curious sense that if one watched long enough some pattern of behaviour would emerge, that one would distinguish various sorts of builders, as one does various sorts of bees.

On the other side of the bridge are two solid, permanent-looking sheds, with perpetual smoke coming from their chimneys, even in high summer. But they are certainly not large enough to hold the crowds of men who make up this constant bridge traffic, and I used to wonder where they all went until I saw that they all go into the war-damaged houses on either side of the cellar. It is clear that no ordinary work is being done here, for the scaffolding and heaps of sand outside the houses are exactly the same in January as in July.

What are they doing? I believe I have discovered the answer. I believe I have stumbled on one of the most arcane mysteries of this literal freemasonry; for nearly every evidence shows that this is not really a building site at all but a school of magic and deportment for young builders. I have observed that in the lunch hour the builders are all young men, of nineteen or twenty, who play soccer with a little ball; yet the same men seen moving gravely across the bridge could not possibly be a day under fifty-five.

Clearly, on this site the men are being schooled in the grave behaviour of builders before the public, and the war-damaged houses contain theoretical classrooms where the more secret parts of the syllabus are taught. The first lesson of the day is always Heap Changing, in which a heap of tubular scaffolding is thrown, piece by piece, into another heap – or sometimes, judging by the sound, into a deep pit. This is followed by exercises in Baulk Banging, and later in the morning the students may be seen in the Balancing Class, walking about with various heavy objects on their heads.

The more advanced training, in the classrooms, is hidden from the public. There is, for instance, Materials Transformation, or Reverse Building, in which the students really come to grips with the unreality of materials. All that the public actually sees is enormous lorries, their red doors bearing the name of some firm of brothers in dockland, which arrive with loads of bricks or tiles; these heaps are later simply spirited away. We never see the stuff being carried into the houses. One moment it is there, and the next time we look it isn't.

Fires and hoists play an important part in building ritual, and at the *collegium* there is an incessant commerce of buckets between some men with a mobile vat containing a perfect Etna of boiling tar and some more men on the roof. They cannot have been putting tar on the roof all this time, for by now it would have been two feet thick. Obviously, the buckets of tar are sent down again by hoist on the other side of the house; the real reason for this is to give instruction not only in deportment before the public but also in Builders' Cries, such as HOINALOINABUR! and GROYT! If the reader will utter these words in a high, strangled voice he will see what I mean, although not what the builders mean.

At night the mysteries are guarded with cumbersome red votive lamps and an old man who, like the Porter in the Rule of St Benedict, 'knoweth how to give and receive an answer'.

SMALL RALLY NOT HELD

'Money,' said Emerson, 'is as beautiful in its operations and effects as roses.' The more I see of economic writing, the more I am convinced that the financial world is streaked with poetry. One of the poet's gifts is condensation, the ability to pack overtones into a title, or even a headline, and I first noticed this gift in economists when, a long time ago, I read for an examination a book called *The Mechanism of Exchange* by John L. Todd.

It was not one of your simplified books, with diagrams containing those little rows of cement statues with bowler hats (or skirts) with only one arm and one leg of the last one showing. It was a proper textbook; and it had those marginal headlines, just like *The Ancient Mariner*. 'The Issue Department', they said, and 'Relieving the Discount Market', and, more rhetorically, 'The Hub of the Universe' – this turned out to be the Bank of England.

Economist friends tell me that this book is now out of date. But it served to introduce me to the fascinating study of the headlines of City Pages. I have found that these cover the whole range of human emotions, from ecstasy ('Rails Soar') to despair and chaos ('Wall Street Plunges'). The virtue to which they return again and again is the Roman Stoic one of Steadiness, and where they are really at their best is in conveying this steadiness when it is tinged with a gentle, autumnal melancholy, reminding one of the Stoics holding on to their rewardless virtues in the sad sunset of humanism as the empire broke up. Recently I have collected three superlative examples in this genre – 'Middle Wits Decline', 'Quiet Tin

Market' and, most poignant of all, 'Small Rally Not Held'.
'Middle Wits Decline' might well be a part of the famous
Yeats poem:

> Things fall apart: the centre cannot hold;
> Mere anarchy is loosed upon the world,
> The blood-dimmed tide is loosed, and everywhere
> The ceremony of innocence is drowned;
> Middle wits decline ...

Do you not see these middle wits, asked long ago to the
bright dinner parties of Barons, famous for their moderate,
restrained, civilized jests, now sitting in silent senility, like
the Senate in empty Rome when the Gauls came? Or perhaps
they are sitting, haunted with memories, in the Quiet Tin
Market, where dusty sunbeams filter past portraits of mighty,
long-forgotten tin merchants stretching right back to Phoeni-
cian days; where dusty piles of ingots dwarf the few low-
voiced men conducting the puny tin business of today.

But it is 'Small Rally Not Held' that haunts me. City Page
headlines often do not hesitate to break away from purely
financial matters and consider the larger social scene; and here
we have an unforgettable picture of a small town, where for
weeks they have been planning their rally, largely because
there has always been one every year before.

This time, as the organizers walk round the small triangular
field behind the gasworks, deciding where the tea marquee
shall be, arguing over the expense of hiring the silver band
from the larger town eleven miles away, a dreadful inertia
begins to take hold of them. Sadly, they know that the world
is changing, that a silver band playing 'Poet and Peasant' is
not sophisticated enough for young people who hear
American bands every week at the Kapitol Kinema. But the
arrangements go forward, although hardly any tickets are sold
yet. 'They'll all come on the day,' the Secretary tells the Rally
Committee with forced cheerfulness.

When the day comes it is pouring with rain. The bands-
men's bus swishes wetly up the street of little houses towards
the rally field. Stewards in dripping mackintoshes with arm-

bands direct all the participants into the hall of the Council School (A.D. 1894 it says in a stone diamond in the wall) opposite. Schoolchildren, leaving their sodden banners in the porch, crowd in to be told that the rally is postponed until three o'clock. But after an uncertain morning of cheese sandwiches and weak, unsugared tea, it is raining as hard as ever ...

No, it is all too terrible. One can only hope that they were consoled by being reported in a national newspaper.

ALFA BRAVO OVER

Something has happened to toys, you no longer get the feeling that they are made by little old men with glasses on the ends of their noses, in some place like Nuremberg. Toys have gone industrial, they use plastics; chemists who know all about dichlorotricyclbicyclpolyputaketlon are involved in their manufacture. They have gone serious – or industry has gone frivolous. Somewhere, in some serious-looking factory, draughtsmen, fitters, shop stewards, storemen, have been concerned in making, for instance, an insane-looking marsupial, dressed in blue bathing trunks and a Cambridge scarf with red tassels, which sits on a wheeled platform. In front of it is a xylophone containing three tuneless notes; and when this contraption is pulled along, the animal, staring madly out of its four eyes (for it is painted on both sides), beats dementedly at this instrument with its spring arms. It sounds like a Balinese orchestra being pulled on a porter's trolley at Euston.

Someone must have taken a drawing of this creature into a superior's office. He would look at it in silence, then say 'I think you've got something there, Carter' – adding, with the irresistible urge of all executives to make 'creative' amendments, 'I think you'd better give him a little red skull cap, like *this*.' Then, briskly flipping an intercom switch: 'Alastair, get on to Jobson and Tukes, ask them to quote for 10,000 xylophone notes, urgentest. And send Hawkins up, we'll have to re-jig No. 2. . . .'

Actually this thing is made of wood, a traditional material much closer to Nuremberg than most of the toys which apppeared in my house this Christmas. Consider, for instance, the Bubble Boy Bandsman. This is a plastic homuncule obviously turned out as mechanically as a carburettor (more mechanically, when you think of all those fiddling little screws and washers and springs in a carburettor, I bet *they're* put in by little old men, probably watchmakers). Indeed the Bubble Boy has some resemblance to a carburettor, for inside the pink saxophone he is holding is a complicated plastic mechanism of pipes and rings, and what you are supposed to do is to *pour small amount of bubble mixture into open end of saxophone and then press Bubble Boy's hat* (he is wearing a rubber bowler) *and watch bubbles appear*. But however hard we pressed nothing happened except a lot of clicking and gurgling, and presently bubble mixture began to ooze out through his boots.

Then there was the Dan Dare Interplanetary Walkie-Talkie. This should really be called a Sittie-Talkie, for it is just two plastic telephones connected by wire. Like all the industrial toys, it was a bit advanced for our children, since the eldest is four. But my friend Harblow and I had a wonderful time. He went into the kitchen with one telephone, I stayed in the drawing-room with the other:

ME: It says here you have to say 'Over' otherwise your friend won't know when to move it from his mouth to his ear. Can you hear me, friend? Over.

HARBLOW [*very faint*]: Table cake arresting, table cake arresting, table cake arresting. . . .

ME: We'll never get anywhere if you don't say 'Over'. Remember Signals Procedure. Over.

HARBLOW [*complete silence. Then a far-away blowing, then a sound like a tin mouse whistling. Suddenly Harblow appears at the door*]: I can't hear a thing.

ME: You were listening while I was waiting for you to talk. I heard *you*. What was all that about table cake arresting?

HARBLOW: I said Able Baker Testing. Able Baker Testing.

ME: They've changed it since our day, it's Alfa Bravo now.

HARBLOW: What, again?

ME: But you still have to say 'Over'. Now, you go back, and I'll speak first. [*Exit Harblow. I read from box*] Rotate planet 59 deg. E. on 'N' axis and attack with full force of Disintegrators. Over.

HARBLOW [*still very faint*]: Hah, ha, ha [*Shrieks of laughter.*] Over.

ME: You're very faint. Over.

HARBLOW [*roaring*]: Alfa Bravo, Alfa Bravo, Alfa Bravo, what do they mean, Alfa, not Bravo at all. Over.

ME: I can hear your real voice above the telephone now. Hold it very close and whisper.

HARBLOW: You forgot to say 'Over'. Over.

ME: Sorry, over. Over.

HARBLOW: I say what did the umpire say when he lost count. He said, Is the over over? Over. Hahaha, over over, over. Over.

ME: That wasn't whispering. Over.

HARBLOW [*surprisingly*]: I say, can you bring a hairpin over? Over.

HARBLOW [*complete silence*].

The silence went on for so long that I borrowed a hairpin from my wife and went into the kitchen. It was full of bubbles. Harblow was pressing the Bubble Boy's hat, his saxophone was belching bubbles.

'You had the jet clogged,' said Harblow. 'I've cleared it with this paper clip.'

INTOURIST ON CAPITAL

Here's a wonderful holiday for those who delight in the novel and intriguing – a trip to Moscow, exciting exotic city of contrasts! Fiery Cossack, stocky Slav, inscrutable Chinese – all are to be found thronging the streets ... there are all kinds of sports for you to watch or take part in, too – soccer, volleyball, swimming, and horse-racing, for instance
– *B.E.A. 1960 holiday booklet*

A wide street in Moscow. Among the gay crowds are Mr Benson Russell, an insurance manager from Ealing, and his wife. Coming here was her idea; he would have preferred to take the car somewhere near St Tropez. They have stopped to sit on a stone bench beneath a rugged statue of some kind of intellectual.

MRS: That looks extraordinarily like Jung to me. You remember, he was on the television.

MR: I expect it *is* Jung. They have collective farms, why not the collective unconscious?

MRS: Do you think this is the way to Intourist?

MR: That'll be the day, when they have another organization for Russian tourists going abroad, called Outtourist.

MRS: What's the matter with you? You're simply making no effort. Why didn't you listen to First Steppes in Russian on Network Three, like me?

MR: All right then. Ask me a question.

MRS: What are the chief towns of the Kirghiz Republic?

MR: Frunze, Karakol, Osh, Dmitrievsk, and Tulcha. I wish we could go to Osh. I bet it's more fun there.

[*A stilyagi, or Russian teddy boy, sidles up to them*].

STILYAGI: You wish to dash to Osh, tosh?

MR: Yesh. In a droshky. A Coshack droshky.

STILYAGI: Have you nylons, cameras, copies of *Lolita*, records of Gershom Parkington Quintet, English Palm Court jazz? I buy pants off you, ha ha very fonny.

A GIRL STUDENT: Do not listen to him, Comrade Englishman. He is *ne-kulturny*, a worthless parasite corrupted by the bourgeois West. Let us exchange information about our two great countries. How many debtors have you in the Fleet prison? Long live peace!

MRS: Comrade Student, we don't have debtors any more, we have hire-purchase.

MR: In England the motorists are oppressed. Death to the hyena Marples. [*Recklessly*] What about the kulaks?

CROWD: ¡ƎᴚⱯᗺUHᴚ ¡ƎᴚⱯᗺUHᴚ

MRS: Ah, Benson, wild, headstrong Benson, am I fated to be forever rescuing you from your wild scrapes?

[*Goes off in search of the Intourist man. When she returns with him the near-riot caused by Benson Russell has turned into a game of volleyball. This is a breathless, scrambling affair in which a formless crowd on either side of a high net slam a great flabby ball about (it seems to have seeds inside it) with their wrists. There is always some leaping show-off on your side who gets to the ball before you do, except when a giant on the other side slams it straight at you, in which case you slam it back with a shock that numbs you up to the shoulder, but it nevertheless flumps into the net in a porridgey sort of way. Here, they have the net right across the wide street; there are about 200 persons on each side. Benson Russell has just slammed the ball into the net.*]

AN INSCRUTABLE CHINESE: Velly silly volley, cully. Bally silly.

INTOURIST MAN: Perhaps the comrade sporting tourists would care to try horse-racing?

[*All adjourn to a near-by race-course. Horses are provided for the Benson Russells, the inscrutable Chinese, a stocky Slav, and a fiery Cossack, from whom Mrs Benson Russell, who hacks on Ealing Common at weekends, wins by a short head.*]

INTOURIST MAN: Now we allot handicaps. It was a draw. Everybody won. Long live collective horse-racing.

MRS: I say, that's not fair. I won!

CROWD: ¡ꓭꓤAꓭꓴHꓤ ¡ꓭꓤAꓭꓴHꓤ

MR: Ah well, you can't expect to get owt for knout, old girl.

INTOURIST MAN: How about some soccer now?

MR: Ah, yes. Volleyball's not really my game, you know. But I don't think I'd be up to the Dynamos.

INTOURIST MAN: Oh, we have just the thing, two small local teams, the Armatures and the Commutators.

MRS: Well, I'm going swimming with this fiery Cossack. I'll meet you outside that department store, by Gum.

MR: By Gum. What a novel and intriguing holiday!

STOPPING AND MOWING

(Instructions that should have come with my motor mower)

We welcome you to the ranks of satisfied owners of Motor Mowers. Well, 'ranks' is hardly the word, you think you're an officer now you've got one of these, don't you, ha ha! Just because your lawn is a bit bigger than the average suburban size, you see yourself gently ambling behind the thing, painting a swathe of perfect greensward as you go....

Who do you think you are? This is the cheapest model we make, all gaudily painted to attract people like you. You must know that proper lawns, belonging to stately homes or golf clubs, are mowed with proper, *dark green* mowers, that the man sits on in a shiny steel saddle; old mowers, that we made fifty years ago, efficient, heavy, inherited by their owners, long before these modern notions of egalitarianism and an expanding economy compelled us to turn out these fiddling little things for people like you, to keep our factory going in off-periods, when we are not servicing these proper, old mowers for out titled clients. However, since you've bought it, and much good may it do you, here are a few hints.

STARTING (*a*) From cold:

1. Take the plug out. Watch that little tin thing sticking up; it catches your knuckles when the spanner suddenly gives. We've given you a set of spanners, made of lead.

2. Clean the plug, if possible. It will be smothered in oil, because you have to put the oil in the petrol; there is no separate lubrication system. *You* probably think the oil is ignited with the petrol vapour in the cylinder, so how can

158

you lubricate an engine with smoke? Well, as you can see, it isn't ignited. It just wets the plug.

3. Undo the nut at the bottom of the cylinder, and a lot more oil will dribble out – well, you shouldn't *have* it on the grass yet. Put the nut back – steady, not too tight, the bottom of the cylinder is made of lead, too. Well, now you've broken the thread, just make it as tight as you can.

3a. You've left the washer off that nut. That's why you broke the thread. No garage will have a washer that size, you'd better start looking for it in the grass.

4. Put plug back, and watch out for your other knuckles. Aah, sorry! The same knuckles. Not too tight, you won't get away with doing this just once, you'll only make it hard to undo again.

5. Kick starter (or pull rope, if it's one of those). Again. Full choke. Again, again, again. Full throttle. Again twenty-seven times, with every possible combination of throttle and choke with half thrott --

6. Switch the petrol on, you fool.

7. Repeat (5). Then repeat (1–4), plug will be wetter than when you started by now.

8. Repeat (5) again. Go and lie down for a bit.

9. Run like hell with it in gear.

STARTING (*b*) From hot:

It is impossible to start this engine from hot. It is something to do with that oil vapour. Once you let it stop, you've had it, you'll have to wait for it to get stone-cold and start from the beginning. Just don't leave it for a second, and keep it roaring.

ADJUSTMENT OF BLADES:

There is a hairbreadth adjustment on this machine, between the position where it just brushes the top of the grass and the one where it digs great gashes in the earth. Practise with a new electric light switch. If you can find a position where the light just flickers between 'on' and 'off ' you'll be able to wangle these blades. Remember that they are finely, not to say neurotically adjusted. Quite a small pebble will wrench the blades out of shape. You will know when this has happened when they either make a frightful clanging noise or won't go round at all. The people for whom we make our proper mowers do not have pebbles on their lawns, let alone the small metal fire engines, dolls' boots, plastic alphabets, nails, and spoons that litter yours.

OPERATION:

It is only possible to operate this machine at a *steady trot*. At ordinary walking pace it will stall. And remember, the clutch is not a gradual affair like the one on a car. The instant you engage it the machine will rush away, with or without you. So it's no good trying to cut round those silly little circular rosebeds you have. This machine only mows in a dead straight line, any curves and you'll dig into the earth. What do you expect for the price you paid, a differential axle?

MAINTENANCE:

You will find a number of little contraptions with spring caps, for putting the oil in. They won't leave room for the spout of any oilcan, however thin; you'll just have to squirt away, making an oozy mess, and hope some of it's getting in. Soon the spring caps will come off, anyway; then there'll just be these little holes, blocked with oily grass.

Finally, three golden rules:

1 Keep a magnet for finding washers, spring caps, nuts, etc.

2 NEVER LET IT STOP.

3 Don't give your hand-mower away.

JUST A FEW FRIENDS

I once heard a lady, discussing who should be invited to a party, say, 'Oh, don't let's have him. He's always the Life and Soul.' This lady was on a bus, so I couldn't hear any more of her views about the ideal guest. But it set me thinking. Normally, when one gives a party, one simply asks all one's friends: one never remembers, in the enthusiasm of preparation, that friends who are perfectly all right individually somehow come out quite different at a party. No matter whether it's one's own party or someone else's (with, presumably, a different lot of friends), there seems to be something about parties that makes certain definite types emerge. The Life and Soul is only one of them, but let's start with him. (Note: M and W stand for Man and Woman.)

THE LIFE AND SOUL (M)

For a long time I used to think that being a Life and Soul was an affliction with which people were born. I noticed they all had those popping-out eyes, probably something to do with the thyroid gland. You could tell a Life and Soul right at the beginning of a party, before he had got around to the tricks with glasses of water, or organizing that exhausting polo where people sit astride chairs and ride them about using an orange as a ball and teaspoons as sticks. Long before that, you found yourself in a group with this Life and Soul; perhaps you were telling some mild story of a minor motor accident in which you were involved. This Life and Soul would listen with barely concealed impatience and then tell you about his

Accident; but in the car that hit him was the Egyptian Ambassador, or Marlene Dietrich, or the Lord Mayor of Liverpool. And when they started surveying the damage, who should have been passing by as a witness but ... well, I needn't go on.

ZOMBIES (M or W)

It was when I became aware of this type, which is the opposite of the Life and Soul, that I first became uneasily aware that a quite normal party guest could be forced into being a Life and Soul. (You know what a zombie is, it's something to do with West Indian voodoo, a corpse being used by a demon or somebody else's soul or something; a terrible kind of straw person who just stares at you with dead eyes.) Suppose one were at a party of those zombies, suppose one came in and the whole room was utterly silent, with these zombies knocking back martinis? Ah, you say, zombies don't drink. But they do. In pubs or restaurants, I have seen couples, or even groups of friends, sitting in complete silence for an hour over their drinks. They get up together, as if at some wordless signal, and go off to who knows what noiseless household, almost as if they lived under the sea. If these people can drink, they can give parties, and it's not beyond the law of averages that one should find oneself a guest thereat. Then one would only have to remark that it looked like rain, and they would tell each other (or, more likely, write each other little notes saying) 'that chap thinks he's the Life and Soul. ...'

I've never actually been to a party full of zombies, but there are always one or two. And I don't know whether I have a kind face or what, but the hostess usually says to me, 'Do go and talk to so and so', and there is this limp-looking character, who gives me a boneless handshake and says absolutely nothing. At first I talk reasonably, then more and more wildly, unable to stop my own voice, hypnotized by the terrible silence. Still, I think I prefer the zombie to

THE ARGUER (M usually)

This type has an awful knack of steering conversation into controversial channels. He will seize some trifling remark and issue a challenge about it. Suppose the talk is about a radio, for instance, and someone admits he hasn't got a licence for his. Not boastingly: he simply admits he's always meant to, but has never got around to it. The Arguer then says, 'But I thought you were religious.'

'I don't know about religious,' says the other diffidently, 'I go to church, yes.'

'Well, I don't know,' says the Arguer, pretending to be all innocent and perhaps-I've-got-this-wrong-but-do-tell-me, 'I've always thought religious people had this terrific *light* inside. I mean, I'm not accusing you of being dishonest, but I simply don't see how you can square not having a wireless licence with the Ten Commandments and all that; of course, I'm not religious myself ...' And so on, and in no time his unfortunate companion is involved in an intense, ding-dong argument about the Nature of the Universe: all right in its place, but not at a party.

Quite often the Arguer is also

THE STAYER (M)

simply because no one can think how to break the argument off. But not necessarily. The Stayer seems unable to drag himself away from any party.

There always comes a time when the hostess, seeing that only this Stayer and three or four of her intimate friends remain among the littered ashtrays and empty glasses, has to invite them all to bacon and eggs in the kitchen. And mention of ashtrays reminds me of

THE DESTROYERS (M and W)

Perhaps the most common type of all. No matter how many chairs you provide they always sit on the edge of a little table and knock sherry on to the carpet. They take a startled step forward, or backward, and you hear the glass snap under their foot. And I don't need to tell you what they do with cigarettes. Then there is

THE TELEPHONE USER (M or W)

It's not that you grudge this person fourpence when he says, 'Do you mind if I use your phone?' He asks so earnestly that you think it must be some terribly important deal he has to close. But you are vaguely troubled by him half the evening as, sitting down in a corner of the room, one hand pressing his ear to keep out the noise of your guests, he pursues his endless conversation. When there is a sudden silence in the room he (or she) is heard saying, 'But darling, you know we've been over all that.' Everybody starts talking again.

THE BRINGER OF A FRIEND (W)

on the other hand, never bothers to telephone you and ask if you'd mind if they brought Fred or Carol who, for some mysterious reason, cannot be abandoned. Fred or Carol usually turn out to be zombies.

THE OLIVE-AND-NUT-EATER (M, I can't think why)

Most people like to drink at parties, but this type likes to eat. He holds a plate of nuts or olives, eating absent-mindedly all the time, forgetting to pass them round. Then he starts on the canapés, taking all the nice ones first, so that in no time all that's left is the ones with rather hopeless bits of cheese. Still, he's better than

THE DRINKER (M)

This man is all the others, except the zombie, rolled into one. The laughter from his end of the room gets more and more raucous. Being a Stayer, too, instead of accepting the bacon and eggs he wants to take the survivors to a pub. . . .

If the lady on the bus went on to exclude all these types, she'd never have a party at all. And speaking as one who in his time has taken uninvited guests, spilt sherry, and eaten all the nuts, I can't help feeling how much poorer life would be if there were no parties.

TWENTY JOKE MENTHOLS, PLEASE

I suspect that I am not the only man who, every time he buys a packet of cigarettes, thinks of it, sometimes vaguely and sometimes quite resolutely, as the last one. I live permanently in the middle of a three-week period when things are a bit hectic; they've been a bit hectic for ten days, and I should have got through the worst of it in another ten days. Indeed by the time I have got through this very packet I shall be within sight of easier times. I shall be on a calm, sunny plateau of my life. I shall hear again the vast, meaningful harmony of the universe. I shall become real, a holy content will suffuse me. I simply shan't *want* to smoke any more.

So it is quite a pleasant feeling, buying this last packet. It is like saying farewell to a schoolmaster, like buying an enormous meal on the quayside with one's last francs, like shooting grouse on the last day of the season (whenever that is. Everybody knows the Glorious Twelfth, when they start; but when do they finish, when is the Hateful Twenty-seventh or the Gloomy Third?) Ah well, tobacco, you and I have been good friends. ...

In fact, I suffer from a mild delusion that I am giving up smoking all the time. And as with other and more violent delusions, long habituation has enabled me to live a perfectly happy, indeed a rather snug life with two perfectly opposite outlooks. In a way I can quite see what it is like to think, with one part of one's mind, that one is a poached egg, while with another part one does things that one knows quite well no poached egg could attempt, such as playing the piano or getting on a bus. And, just as there must be sudden terrible moments when one stands right outside the whole thing, when one realizes that this whole poached-egg business must cease, so do I experience sudden cold blasts of reality about my non-smoking.

For instance, I have just been shaken by the extraordinary, the idiotic number and variety of articles in the drawer where I keep all my non-smoking devices and subterfuges – things on which I have, for the last two years, been spending money *in addition* to that spent on cigarettes. Somehow I had never noticed them as an aggregate, a collection, before. It was really the addition to them, this week, of my latest failure, a useless little cigarette-rolling machine, which somehow transformed this drawerful into a significant and crazy museum collection. In this drawer, covered with dust, are the following articles:

1. THE THREE EXPENSIVE PIPES

All failures. I tried all kinds of tobacco; light yellow tobacco, and rich dark tobacco smelling of rum, out of cool jars in high-class, eighteenth-century shops. Sometimes it would sizzle and drop red-hot pieces on to my writing pad. Sometimes the smoke got into my eyes, since a pipe cannot be kept out of range, as it were. There is nowhere you can put a pipe down for a second; it falls over on any ashtray. My pipes all filled up rapidly with coke and peat. I spent hours poking in them with peculiar instruments, one of which is incised with the words

2. PIPE REAMER

and I see that in one of the distracted moments of the non-smoker I have scratched another letter so that it now says Pipe Dreamer.

3. THE GREAT BAG OF HERBS

This is the remains of an ounce of some medical mixture
I once tried. It said in the advertisement it was good for
asthma. I haven't got asthma, so I reasoned it would be even
better for me. It looks like dried lavender and pounded birds'
nests, and when first lit causes a thin crackling flame to rise
from the pipe. Other people in the room tend to like the
gentle autumn melancholy of its garden-fire smell; but it
burns my tongue.

4. THE GREEN TABLETS

(one after each meal) are supposed to make cigarettes taste
awful. But they make everything else, including my tongue,
nay, my very soul, taste awful as well. Also bad for the tongue
is

5. THE JOKE MENTHOL CIGARETTE

since the air hole in the celluloid thing holding the crystals
lets them escape into my mouth. I don't think one should
eat menthol. The black holder contains a rather childishly
crude image of a half-burnt cigarette, with a sort of tiny stage
fire at the end, red paper and bright aluminium-powder ashes.

6. THE CIGARETTE MACHINE

makes even more extraordinary cigarettes than the ones I
tried to roll by hand. No two are the same. Some are
convex, some are concave, like a tiny pillow with all the
stuffing pushed out of the middle; some are tapering. Some
burn half-way down the moment I light them, others are as
solid as pencils and require to be sucked until blue lights
dance before my eyes, otherwise they go out. All have loose
ends, all come unstuck on my lips.

7. LIQUORICE ALL-SORTS, LEMON SHERBETS, BARLEY SUGAR, CURIOUSLY STRONG PEPPERMINTS

like all concentrated foods, induce a feeling of repletion and the desire to smoke.

In fact all these things, in their various ways, stimulate a desire for cigarettes. I must cut down on them.

S TIMES WHAT?

I do wish that the people who write about Britain's need for scientists would stop saying that our traditional bias towards the Classics means that science is non-U and that science students are looked down on. Goodness, how hopelessly I used to envy and admire those boys, with propelling pencils that they never lost, and two fountain pens – worn, neat, *old men's* fountain pens, one with red ink in – whose experiments worked, whose results came out right.

They had the right, detached attitude to matter, which is basically white or yellow powder in menacing little bottles. They weren't afraid of breaking it down, whereas I felt, even then, doubtless in a deplorably primitive and superstitious way, that it was best left alone.

Look at salt, creature of innocence, used in baptism. Good old salt, you put it in soup, it's collected from pans in Cheshire. But you break it down (by the Electrolysis of Brine, of course) and, who would have thought it, there is chlorine, a poisonous gas, and sodium, in sticks like awful mouldering Edinburgh rock, you must always add water to it, not it to water – no, wait, I think it's the other way round – sizzle, spurt, cough, heavens, the damn stuff's *on fire, in water*, a science master with bony knuckles is pinching my ear, absolutely convinced I did it on purpose.

And look how frightening it gets when you go farther and break down the sodium and chlorine into all those protons, mesons, crotons, cretins, morons, anti-morons, etc. Those boys with fountain pens that never made blots, those boys whose socks never came down, they could make matter sit up and beg for them. Once we had to grow crystals, we made a saturated solution, I forget how now, on a Friday afternoon, we left our crystals suspended, when we came back on Monday those boys had grown great Koh-i-noor diamonds, but mine had dissolved into a kind of brown porridge.

Those boys knew that beautiful, coordinated relationships existed between one element and another, and between all elements and this sinister, unitary hydrogen. But I could never get the *relationship between the relationships* sorted out – valency, equivalent weight, molecular weight, atomic weight, absolute mass ... those boys, in their experiments, elegantly and systematically removed the layers of ignorance between man and the secret dance of matter, but I found myself drawing elaborate flames coming out of the bunsen burner, or shading to make jars appear round, or, in all those experiments with pins and prisms, drawing a realistic eye (the observer, O), once I put in the whole man's face, and his collar and tie; anything to delay writing up the meaningless jumble of figures into 'results'.

I have just discovered an exercise book labelled 'Physics' that I had in 1933, when I was fourteen. *To find the Refractive Index of a Prism*, I wrote. *A prism was taken* ... I felt then, and I feel now, unhappy about this attempt to be lordly, impersonal. Why beat about the bush, *I* took the prism. Lower down, I wrote *the prism having been taken away, of course*, and 'of course' has been crossed out in red ink by the master. Those boys never wrote 'of course', although they had much more right to.

The book simply ends in mid-air, with *To Find the Specific Heat of Alcohol* ('a calorimeter was taken ...'). At the end of the 'Results' it says *Let sp. heat of water be S. Now* $(S \times 50 \cdot 175) + 6 \cdot 25 = S \times \ldots$ and the master has written ' $= S \times what$?'

$S \times$ what, indeed? At least in those days I knew enough to be able to pick out a calorimeter from all the other stuff – those belljars in which stuff was always being collected by Downward-Displacement, those pipettes I always sucked too hard, getting a bitter mouthful of some lugubrious hydroxide.

But this exercise book doesn't recall to me the shape of a calorimeter. It recalls a fantasy I used to have recently when we lived in Hampstead, in a house from which we could see the Surrey heights. I was always afraid of waking, after a peaceful night, to find water lapping the doorstep. In the morning sun a vast lake shimmers away to the south. Far away is this little island (Sanderstead, would it be?). London, Wembley, the Great West Road, all those technicians, lie fathoms deep. On the larger island of the Chilterns there is an agrarian civilization of stockbrokers; and there are plenty of chairs, still made in the high parts of High Wycombe. But somehow I know it is up to us, in Hampstead and Sanderstead, to get the twentieth century going again.

I construct a rude raft and paddle dreamily southwards over the blue water. Presently I see another raft coming towards me. It is occupied by a man who introduces himself as a Mr Cattermole, of Sanderstead. 'Used to be a regional manager for the Prudential,' he says. 'Frankly, we're in a mess at Sanderstead. No electricity, no telly, no fridges. Mostly retired people, you know. Thought you eggheads at Hampstead might help. British improvisation, what? Think you could rig us up a simple dynamo?'

But I don't know any more than he does. (What *was* Fleming's Right-hand Rule? You hold your right hand like this, SeCond finger is Current's direction if Motion (thuMb) is across Field (first Finger). Or was it the Left hand?) We both paddle back to Hampstead. After eating the fish we have caught *en route* we pore over this precious exercise book, now, together with what we can remember, sole repository of man's scientific achievement. After a long silence Cattermole suddenly says 'Avogadro's Hypothesis. It's beginning to come back. And wasn't there something called the Brown Ring Test?'

'Acid Plus Base Equals Salt Plus Water,' I add, without much hope. It begins to get dark, a wind springs up, it is too rough for Cattermole to get back to Sanderstead; all through the night we try to remember, but it is no good. In the bleary morning I stare at him. 'S times *what*?' I ask for the hundredth time.

Suddenly there is the roar of a powerful engine. 'Are you all right?' shouts a cheerful voice. It is a trim launch, full of men in white coats – those boys, grown up. They were all in some research institute up in the mountains in Wales. They *built* this launch in twelve hours.

Thank goodness.

THE UNTHINKABLE CARRIER

John o' Groats,
South Atlantic
13 November 2000

Strange to think, as one sits under the palm trees gazing at the dolphins in the calm blue waters, how nonsensical that dateline would have seemed in 1960. Strange, also, to realize, amid the happy laughter of our children as the world looks forward eagerly to this most wonderful of all centuries, that less than forty years ago the world was racked by the fear of war. Although the British still knew in their hearts that they were the only people in the world with any common sense (except for that curious aberration at Suez), not many of us said so out loud, feeling that we had lost our nineteenth-century power of imposing this common sense on the world through the Pax Britannica.

Economically, Britain stood hesitating between a Commonwealth with dwindling Imperial Preference and a Common Market run by foreigners with peculiar ideas on the Congo, America, the Polish frontier. An election was fought on the issue of a 'telly in every garage', while America and Russia made bigger and bigger missiles. There seemed to be no leadership, and ...

... and all the time we were working secretly on this superb plan which has brought the world its ardently desired peace.

The scientific committee set up in the last days of the Churchill Government to investigate the possibilities of making Britain float began with three great advantages.

1. *So much of the work had been done already*. The task of

174

cutting Britain loose from the solid earth was a logical follow-up of our advantage in a long history of mining, from the Phoenicians in Cornwall to all that modern coal-and-iron-getting at which we, as pioneers of the Industrial Revolution, had worked longer than any other country. Mining, as Lewis Mumford points out, is, in German, *Abbau* or unbuilding; and the committee found that what with the Cheddar caves, the Yorkshire and Derbyshire potholes, and all these mines, there were already enough 'un-built' parts of Britain for it to be feasible to join them all up and fit them with buoyancy tanks.

2. *Britain's early lead in atomic know-how.* It was widely thought at the time that this, dating from Rutherford's Cambridge experiments, had been lost to Russia and America. But the world learnt otherwise on that extraordinary day in June 1966 when Britain, propelled by the giant atomic engines strategically mounted round her coastline, moved majestically towards the South Atlantic. The essential secrecy was greatly helped by

3. *The absence of a 'middle-class' in scientific knowledge.* Science in Britain has always been sharply divided into geniuses and an uncaring general public. The former were all 'in the know'. The latter were easily lulled by all kinds of explanations of such preparations as could not be hidden. They were perfectly ready to believe that the engines were 'atomic power stations', even though there was plenty of power already and the huge gaunt buildings were all on marshy desolate coasts far from any possible demand for power.

The vast establishment at Harwell was explained away by ingenious stories of 'peaceful application of H-power', complete with hand-outs about temperatures much hotter than the sun obtained for millionths of a second (!) in little glass things. There were even photographs of a circular wooden fantasy (made by a Harwell carpenter) mysteriously called Zeta.

The increasingly frequent window-rattling explosions as the unbuilding was hurried forward with atomic blasting were explained as 'aircraft breaking the sound barrier'; the public were easily convinced that sound travels at over 700 miles an hour, whereas anyone who has observed, say, the time between flash and report of a gun on a quite small sports field might have guessed that in fact it travels very slowly (15·27 miles an hour, in fact). Even the littering of the country with huge machines plainly marked EARTH MOVER only suggested road making.

Now Britain enjoys this scientific extension of her traditional balance-of-power policy, and the world's peace is no longer at the mercy of a few cross-looking American admirals or Russian generals. The world knows that any missile, instantly detected by British radar, would automatically set off the Ultimate Weapon – a 'full speed ahead' order to our mighty atomic engines, causing the country to leap forward at 800 knots and make a tidal wave that only we should survive. Much more than in the nineteenth century, Britain now *is* the British Fleet.

The fears of the Isle of Wight that the tow-chain might break, or the island be used simply to carry the luggage, have long since disappeared (and how happy Ireland, in this Jubilee Year of her President, Dame Siobhan McKenna, now feels as the only island off Europe!). By careful course-plotting we are able to have three crop-growing seasons a year, and we have become a net exporter of food.

The off-shore coal and iron mining rights we have maintained in the old sea area we occupied for so long bring in huge revenues. Our own output, now that the industrial strife of the past, attributed by psychologists to the 'Old Climate', is just a memory, flourishes in the clean air of our healthy sub-tropical climate, which has also made the wonderful sandy beaches of the Northumberland Riviera one of the world's great tourist centres. Our currency is the hardest in the world. . . .

But we should not be too complacent. Our agreement with Japan, whereby she, under licence, keeps the Pacific peace as we keep the Atlantic, has worked splendidly. But we may not always keep this technical lead. There are rumours of an imminent German-inspired break-off of Spain from Europe, and China is known to be experimenting with Korea. A world in which every country was a giant marine nuclear dodgem would be a horrifying thought, reviving the worst fears of the sixties. No doubt, however, Britain would come up with a solution. She usually does.

REPORT ON RESISTENTIALISM*

It is the peculiar genius of the French to express their philosophical thought in aphorisms, sayings hard and tight as diamonds, each one the crystal centre of a whole constellation of ideas. Thus, the entire scheme of seventeenth-century intellectual rationalism may be said to branch out from that single, pregnant saying of Descartes, *'Cogito ergo sum'* – 'I think, therefore I am.' Resistentialism, the philosophy which has swept present-day France, runs true to this aphoristic form. Go into any of the little cafés or *horlogeries* on Paris's Left Bank (make sure the Seine is flowing *away* from you, otherwise you'll be on the Right Bank, where *no* one is *ever* seen) and sooner or later you will hear someone say, *'Les choses sont contre nous.'*

'Things are against us.' This is the nearest English translation I can find for the basic concept of Resistentialism, the grim but enthralling philosophy now identified with bespectacled, betrousered, two-eyed Pierre-Marie Ventre. In transferring the dynamic of philosophy from man to a world of hostile Things, Ventre had achieved a major revolution of thought, to which he himself gave the name 'Resistentialism'. Things (*res*) resist (*résister*) man (*homme*, understood). Ventre makes a complete break with traditional philosophic method. Except for his German precursors, Friedegg and Heidansiecker, all previous thinkers from the Eleatics to Marx have allowed at least some legitimacy to human thought and effort. Some, like Hegel or Berkeley, go

* 1949. Some years before Murphy's Law, Sods' Law etc.

178

so far as to make man's thought the supreme reality. In the Resistentialist cosmology that is now the intellectual rage of Paris Ventre offers us a grand vision of the Universe as One Thing – the Ultimate Thing (*Dernière Chose*). And it is against us.

Two world wars have led to a general dissatisfaction with the traditional Western approach to cosmology, that of scientific domination. In Ventre's view, the World-Thing, to which he sometimes refers impartially as the Thing-World, opposes man's partial *stealing*, as it were, of consciousness – of his dividing it into the separate 'minds' with which human history has made increasingly fatal attempts to create a separate world of men. Man's increase in this illusory domination over Things has been matched, *pari passu*, by the increasing hostility (and greater force) of the Things arrayed against him. Medieval man, for instance, had only a few actual Things to worry about – the lack of satisfactory illumination at night, the primitive hole in the roof blowing the smoke back and letting the rain in, and one or two other small Things like that. Modern, domesticated Western man has far more opportunities for battle-losing against Things – can-openers, collar-studs, chests of drawers, open manholes, shoelaces. . . .

Now that Ventre has done it for us, it is easy to see that the reaction against nineteenth-century idealism begun by Martin Freidegg and Martin Heidansiecker was bound eventually to coalesce with the findings of modern physics in a philosophical synthesis for our time. Since much stress has been laid on the 'scientific' basis of Resistentialism, it will not be out of place here, before passing on to a more detailed outline of Ventre's thought, to give a brief account of those recent developments in physical science which have so blurred the line that separates it from metaphysics. It is an account which will surprise those whose acquaintance with Ventre is limited to reading reviews of his plays and who, therefore, are apt to think that Resistentialism is largely a matter of sitting inside a wet sack and moaning.

A convenient point of departure is provided by the famous Clark-Trimble experiments of 1935. Clark-Trimble was not primarily a physicist, and his great discovery of the Graduated Hostility of Things was made almost accidentally. During some research into the relation between periods of the day and human bad temper, Clark-Trimble, a leading Cambridge psychologist, came to the conclusion that low human dynamics in the early morning could not sufficiently explain the apparent hostility of Things at the breakfast table – the way honey gets between the fingers, the unfoldability of newspapers, etc. In the experiments which finally confirmed him in this view, and which he demonstrated before the Royal Society in London, Clark-Trimble arranged four hundred pieces of carpet in ascending degrees of quality, from coarse matting to priceless Chinese silk. Pieces of toast and marmalade, graded, weighed, and measured, were then dropped on each piece of carpet, and the marmalade-downwards incidence was statistically analysed. The toast fell right-side-up every time on the cheap carpet, except when the cheap carpet was screened from the rest (in which case the toast didn't know that Clark-Trimble had other and better carpets), and it fell marmalade-downwards every time on the Chinese silk. Most remarkable of all, the marmalade-downwards incidence for the intermediate grades was found to vary *exactly* with the quality of carpet.

The success of these experiments naturally switched Clark-Trimble's attention to further research on *resistentia*, a fact which was directly responsible for the tragic and sudden end to his career when he trod on a garden rake at the Cambridge School of Agronomy. In the meantime, Noys and Crangenbacker had been doing some notable work in America. Noys carried out literally thousands of experiments, in which subjects of all ages and sexes, sitting in chairs of every conceivable kind, dropped various kinds of pencils. In only three cases did the pencil come to rest within easy reach. Crangenbacker's work in the social-industrial field, on the relation of human willpower to specific problems such as whether a train or subway will stop with the door opposite you on a crowded platform, or whether there will be a mail box anywhere on your side of the street, was attracting much attention.

Resistentialism, a sombre, post-atomic philosophy of pagan, despairing nobility, advocates complete withdrawal from Things. Now that Ventre has done the thinking for us it is easy to see how the soil was being prepared for Resistentialism in the purely speculative field by the thought of Martin Friedegg (1839–1904) and Martin Heidansiecker (1850–1910), both well-known anti-idealists and anti-intellectualists. It is in the latter's *Werke* (Works) published at Tübingen in 1894, that the word *Resistentialismus* first appears, although it has not the definite meaning assigned to it by Ventre. It is now possible to trace a clear line of development to Ventre from Goethe, who said, with prophetic insight into the hostility of one Thing, at least, 'Three times has an apple proved fatal. First to the human race, in the fall of Adam; secondly to Troy, through the gift of Paris; and last of all, to science through the fall of Newton's apple' (*Werke*, XVI, 17). Later we find Heidansiecker's concept of *Dingenhass*, the hatred of Things. But in the confused terminology of this tortured German mystic we are never sure whether it is Things who hate us, or we who hate the Things.

To the disillusioned youth of post-war France there was an immediate appeal in Ventre's relentlessly logical concept of man's destiny as a *néant*, or No-Thing, and it was the aesthetic expression of this that gave Resistentialism such great popular currency outside the philosophical textbooks. Ventre himself is an extraordinarily powerful dramatist; his first play, *Puits Clos*, concerns three old men who walk ceaselessly round the bottom of a well. There are also some bricks in the well. These symbolize Things, and the old men hate the bricks as much as they do each other. The play is full of their pitiful attempts to throw the bricks out of the top of the well, but they can, of course, never throw high enough, and the bricks always fall back on them. *Puits Clos* has only recently been taken off at the little Théâtre Jambon to make room for another Resistentialist piece by Blanco del Huevo, called *Comment sont les choses?* Del Huevo is an ardent young disciple of Ventre, and in this play, which is also running in London under the title *The Things That Are Caesar*, he makes a very bold step forward in the application of Resistentialist imagery to the theatre. He had made Things the characters, and reduced the human beings to what are known in Resistentialist language as *Poussés*. The nearest English translation that suggests itself for this philosophical term is 'pushed-arounds'.

The chief 'characters' in *Comment sont les choses?* are thus a piano and a medicine cabinet; attached to the piano is *Poussé* Number One – no human beings are given actual names, because names are one of the devices by which man has for so long blinded himself to his fundamental inability to mark himself out from the Universe (*Dernière Chose*). *Poussé* Number One is determined to play the piano, and the piano is determined to resist him. For the first twenty minutes of Act I, he plays a Beethoven sonata up to a certain bar, which always defeats him. He stops, and plays this bar over a hundred times, very slowly. He gets it right. He begins the sonata again and when he gets to this bar he makes the very same mistake. He pours petrol on the piano and is just about to set it on fire when he hears a huge crash from the bathroom, also visible to the audience on the other side of a stage partition.

All this time the medicine cabinet has been resisting the attempts of *Poussé* Number Two to fix it on the wall, and it has now fallen into the bath. *Poussé* Number One who is in love, naturally, with *Poussé* Number Two's wife, *Poussée*, mimes his derision at the woeful lack of manhood of one who cannot even dominate Things to the extent of fixing a medicine cabinet. While he does so, the piano, with the tragic irony of a Greek chorus, speaks of *Poussé* Number One's own *hubris* and insolence in imagining that he can master the piano. *Poussé* Number Two is too busy to retaliate, as he is sweeping up the mess of camphorated oil, essence of peppermint, hair cream, calamine lotion, and broken glass towards the plug end of the bath, meaning to swill them out with hot water. He is desperately anxious to get this done before *Poussée* arrives home. She comes, however, while he is still trying ignominiously to get the bits of glass off one sticky hand with the other sticky hand, the glass then sticking to the other sticky hand and having to be got off with the first sticky hand (a good example of *choses co-rélatives* in the Resistentialist sense). *Poussée* expresses her scorn and asks her husband, all in mime, why he can't play the piano like *Poussé* Number One (who has persuaded her that he can). Eventually she goes out with *Poussé* Number One, and *Poussé* Number Two, exhausted by his labours at the bath, falls into it and into a deep coma.

Act II is extremely unconventional, and although some critics have hailed it as a great attempt to break down the modern separation between players and audience it seems to me to be the weakest part of the play, the nearest to a mere philosophical treatise. The curtain simply goes up on a Resistentialist exhibition, and the audience are invited to walk round. While they are examining the exhibits, which contain not only Resistentialist paintings but also what Ventre as well as Del Huevo calls *objets de vie* (chests of drawers, toothpaste caps, collar buttons, etc.), the stage manager comes on in his shirt sleeves and reads the chapter on sex from Ventre's *Résistentialisme*. Ventre takes a tragic view of sex, concerned as it is with the body, by which the World-Thing obtains its mastery over human territory. In so far as man is not merely a body he is only a pseudo-Thing (*pseudo-chose*), a logical 'monster'. Ventre sees woman, with her capacity for reproduction indefinitely prolonging this state of affairs, as the chief cause of humanity's present dilemma of Thing-separation and therefore Thing-warfare. Love between humans, i.e. between Man (Not-woman) and Woman (Not-man), perpetuates bodies as Things, because a man, in being a Not-woman, shows the capacity of all things for being only *one* Thing (it is all much clearer in the French, of course). Just as a man is a Not-woman, he is also a Not-sideboard, a Not-airplane. But this is as far as man can go in Thingness, and if it were not for woman we could all die and be merged comfortably in the Universe or Ultimate Thing.

In Act III, the action, if one can call it that, is resumed. When the curtain goes up *Poussé* Number Two is discovered still lying in the bath. The tragedy of man's futile struggle against the power of Things begins to draw towards its fatal climax as we hear a conversation between the piano and the medicine cabinet in which the piano suggests an exchange of their respective *Poussés*. The piano, realizing that *Poussée* doesn't know anything about music anyway and will probably accept *Poussé* Number One's word that he can play, queering the pitch for Things with this ambivalent concept of love, wishes to lure Number Two on instead. (In Ventre's system, Things are quite capable of emanations and influences by reason of their affinity with man's Thing-Body or Not-other.) Accordingly, when *Poussé* Number Two wakes up in the bath he feels a compulsive desire to play the piano, forgetting that his fingers are still sticky – and of course it is not his piano anyway. The piano, biding its time, lets him play quite well. (In Resistentialist jargon, which unashamedly borrows from the terminology of Gonk and others when necessary, the resistance of the I-Thing is infinite and that of the Thou-Thing is zero – it is always *my* bootlaces that break – and of course *Poussé* Number Two thinks he is playing Poussé Number One's piano.) Number Two only leaves the instrument when he hears the others coming back. He goes to the bathroom and listens through the partition with a knowing smile as *Poussé* Number One begins to play for *Poussée*. Naturally, *his* fingers stick to the keys the piano being an I-Thing for him, or so he thinks. This makes *Poussé* Number Two feel so good that he actually manages to fix the medicine cabinet. *Poussée*, returning to him disillusioned from the pseudo-pianist, flings herself into his arms, but it is too late. He has cut an artery on a piece of the broken glass sticking out of the medicine cabinet. In despair she rushes back to the music room, where *Poussé* Number One has just lit a cigarette to console himself and think out the next move. ('As if that mattered,' says the piano scornfully.) As she comes in there is a great explosion. *Poussé* Number One has forgotten the petrol he had poured on the piano in Act I.

The drama is not the only art to have been revivified in France (and therefore everywhere) by Resistentialism. This remorseless modern philosophy has been reflected in the work of all the important younger composers and painters in Paris. Resistentialist music, based on acceptance of the tragic Thing-ness, and therefore limitation, of musical instruments, makes use of a new scale based on the Absolute Mathematical Reluctance of each instrument. The A.M.R. of the violin, for instance, is the critical speed beyond which it is impossible to play it because of the strings' melting. The new scale is conceived, says Dufay, as 'a geometric rather than a tonic progression. Each note is seen as a point on the circumference of a circle of which the centre is the A.M.R. The circle must then be conceived as *inside-out*.' Dufay has expressed in mathematical terms that cosmic dissatisfaction of the artist with the physical medium in which he is forced to work. Kodak, approaching the problem from a different angle, has taken more positive steps to limit the 'cosmic offence-power' of the conventional scale by *reducing* the number of notes available. His first concerto, for solo tympanum and thirty conductors, is an extension of the argument put forward some years ago, in remarkable anticipation of Resistentialism, by Ernest Newman, music critic of the London *Sunday Times*, who said that the highest musical pleasure was to be derived much more from score-reading than from actual performance. Kodak is now believed to be working on a piece for conductors only.

I have left Resistentialism in painting to the end because it is over the quarrel between Ventre and Agfa, at one time his chief adherent among the artists, that the little cafés and bistros of the Quartier Latin are seething today. When Agfa first came under Ventre's influence he accepted the latter's detachment, not so much Franciscan as Olympic, from Things. His method was to sit for hours in front of a canvas brooding over disasters, particularly earthquakes, in which Things are hostile in the biggest and most obvious way. Sometimes he would discover that the canvas had been covered during his abstraction, sometimes not. At any rate,

Agfa enjoyed a *succès fou* as a painter of earthquakes and recently he has shown himself impatient of the thorough-going *néantisme* (no-thingery) of Ventre, who insists relentlessly that to conform completely to the pure Resistentialist ideal a picture should not only have no paint but should be without canvas and without frame, since, as he irrefutably points out, these Things are all Things (*ces choses sont toutes des choses*).

The defection of Agfa and of other 'moderates' among the Resistentialists has been brought to a head by the formation, under a thinker named Qwertyuiop, of a neo-Resistentialist group. The enthusiasm with which medieval students brawled in the streets of Paris over the Categories of Being has lost none of its keenness today, and the recent pitched battle between Ventristes and followers of Qwertyuiop outside the Café aux Fines Herbes, by now famous as Ventre's head-quarters, has, if nothing else, demonstrated that Paris still maintains her position as the world's intellectual centre. It is rather difficult to state the terms of the problem without using some of the Resistentialists' phraseology, so I hope I may be pardoned for briefly introducing it.

Briefly, the issue is between Ventre, the pessimist, and Qwertyuiop, the optimist. Ventre, in elaborating on his central aphorism, *les choses sont contre nous*, distinguishes carefully between what he calls *chose-en-soi*, the Thing in itself, and *chose-pour-soi*, the Thing *for* itself. *Chose-en-soi* is his phrase for Things existing in their own right, sublimely and tragically independent of man. In so far as Ventre's pregnant terminology can be related to traditional western categories, *chose-en-soi* stands for the Aristotelean outlook, which tends to ascribe a certain measure of reality to Things without reference to any objective Form in any mind, human or divine. There are even closer parallels with the later, medieval philosophy of Nominalism, which says, roughly, that there are as many Things as we can find names for; Ventre has an interesting passage about what he calls inversion (*inversion*) in which he exploits to the full the contrast between the multiplicity of actions which Things can perform against us – from a slightly overhanging tray falling off a table when the removal of one lump of sugar over-balances it, to the atomic bomb – and the paucity of our vocabulary of names on such occasions.

The third great concept of Ventre is *le néant* (the No-Thing). Man is ultimately, as I have said, a No-Thing, a metaphysical monster doomed to battle, with increasing non-success, against real Things. Resistentialism, with what Ventre's followers admire as stark, pagan courage, bids man abandon his hopeless struggle.

Into the dignified, tragic, Olympian detachment of Ventre's 'primitive' Resistentialism the swarthy, flamboyant Qwertyuiop has made a startling, meteoric irruption. Denounced scornfully by the Ventristes as a plagiarist, Qwertyuiop was, indeed, at one time a pupil of Ventre. He also asserts the hostility of Things to man – but he sees grounds for hope in the concept of *chose-pour-soi* (the Thing for itself) with which it is at least possible to enter into relationships. But he is more a dramatist than a philosopher, and what enrages the Ventristes is the bouncing optimism of his plays and also the curious symbolic figure of the *géant* or giant which appears in them all. This *géant* is a kind of Resistentialist version of Nietzsche's superman, a buskined, moustachioed figure who intervenes, often with great comic effort, just when the characters in the play are about to jump down a well (the well is, of course, a frequent Resistentialist symbol – cf. Ventre's own *Puits Clos*).

The Ventristes point out acidly that in the first edition of *Résistentialisme* the word *géant* appears throughout as a misprint for *néant*. Friction between the two groups was brought to a head by Qwertyuiop's new play *Messieurs, les choses sont terribles*, (loosely, *Gentlemen, Things are Terrible*). On the first night at the Théâtre des Somnambules, the Ventristes in the gallery created an uproar and had to be expelled when, at the end of the second act, the inevitable *géant* had stepped in to prevent three torturings, seven betrayals, and two suicides. The battle was renewed later with brickbats and bottles when Qwertyuiop and his followers interrupted one of Ventre's *choseries*, or Thing-talks, at the Café aux Fines Herbes. Five of the moderates and two Ventristes were arrested by the gendarmerie and later released on bail. All Paris is speculating on the outcome of the trial, at which many important literary figures are expected to give evidence.

It is, however, not in the law courts that the influence of Resistentialism on our time will be decided. It is in the little *charcuteries* and *épiceries* of the Left Bank. It is in the stimulating mental climate of Paris that the artists and dramatists will decide for themselves whether there is any future for art in the refined philosophical atmosphere to which Ventre's remorseless logic would have them penetrate. Although Qwertyuiop has succeeded in attracting many of Ventre's more lukewarm followers among the arts, who had begun to rebel against the Master's uncompromising insistence on pictures without paint and music without instruments, without any Things at all, there seems no doubt that Ventre is the greater thinker, and it is an open question whether he will achieve his object of persuading the world to abandon Things without the indispensable help of the artistic confraternity in moulding public opinion.

There is no doubt, either, that Ventre's thought strikes a deep chord in everyone during these sombre, post-atomic times. Ventre has, I think, liberated the vast flood of creative hatred which makes modern civilization possible. My body, says Ventre, is *chose-en-soi* for me, a Thing which I cannot control, a Thing which uses me. But it is *chose-pour-soi* for the Other. I am thus a Hostile Thing to the Other, and so is he to me. At the same time it follows (or it does in the French) that I am a No-Thing to the world. But I cannot be united or merged with the World-Thing because my Thing-Body, or Not-Other, gives me an illicit and tragically deceptive claim on existence and 'happiness'. I am thus tragically committed to extending the area of my always illusory control over the Thing-body – and as the 'mind' associated with my Thing-body is merely the storing up of recollected struggles with Things, it follows that I cannot know the Other except as one of the weapons with which the World-Thing has increased its area of hostile action.

Resistentialism thus formalizes hatred both in the cosmological and in the psychological sphere. It is becoming generally realized that the complex apparatus of our modern life – the hurried meals, the dashing for trains, the constant meeting of people who are seen only as 'functions': the bar-man, the wife, etc. – could not operate if our behaviour were truly dictated by the old, reactionary categories of human love and reason. This is where Ventre's true greatness lies. He has transformed, indeed reversed the traditional mechanism of thought, steered it away from the old dogmatic assump-tion that we could use Things, and cleared the decks for the evolution of the Thing-process without futile human opposition. Ventre's work brings us a great deal nearer to the realization of the Resistentialist goal summed up in the words, 'Every Thing out of Control.'

FINNEGAN'S SLEEP

A doctor has recently announced that the only possible explanation for a mother's instinctive knowledge of the needs of her child is telepathy. As this would all be down in the subconscious I can't help feeling that the idiom of James Joyce might well be adapted to give a word-picture of what the *baby* thinks. This is what I think one of ours was transmitting when we took him into a restaurant for lunch.

Caverny *Averni facilis* greygloom glugmurk where am I, danger strangers shadowmumbling ominous homines othering me. Smother. O mother, caution required cushioning neverleaving loving abandon *ogni speranza* where am I? Her leaving. Off an orphan. Keep close, sunder a blunder of.
> *They find a table and put him*
> *in a high chair.*

Glugmurch foodfare gobbling globules gluggery goo. O the starch and milching mallecho. Where is intakeintakeintake? Aaaaarhglurch rumble gumble BRING stave starvation of. Rolypoly gammon spinach ch ch tch cram with eels stuffmaw grabcake bungitin voidroaring. Avora devora voracivora; crummy crammy gimme gimme the hymn is why we waiter waiter waiter winterwarmer waita wanta waaaaaaaagh.
> *They give him a piece of bread.*

Graceyous sustentment. Blessyer treasure it's nibble at his nodules. Mumpy noodle a nice, a chumpa champion a champa mmmm.

> *He observes the table, with many*
> *bright knives and forks.*

Crackalight attackabang alotta bright bits agrabba bangem
the merry twinkle a blink of them. O the merry manyworld
a crinkle of pieces and scatterthings so brightly there. O
sparkle images. O my manyworld isitreal istrue mystery.
Touchit an grabbit an fondle the thing, dandle in hand.
Grabbit an bang in hand, grab.

> *He grabs a spoon and bangs on*
> *the table with it.*

A clanka ding dong ting clang. The morningstar. A villainous
Vulcan valhalla hellabang bang clong aging. I'm a god a bang.
Bong. A rhythm a count of number one two bam bam

> *They gently remove the spoon.*

A WOE A WAA A WAE WICTIS. I'm a wictim betrayed
melovely spoonagone.

> *He experimentally pulls table*
> *mat on which are glass, knives,*
> *forks, etc.*

Here's a thing I pull this. Mechanicomiracle, thingpull I
pull it they all come in magictrain. Pull it, impel a pulsion
pushpull. Mechanico-movem. I joy make em move, thisway
thatway, new as Newton's apple a pull a p——

> *They move his high chair out of*
> *range of the table.*

MURDER MAAAA MELOVELY MAT AGONE A MURDER
WAAAAA

> *Waitress appears and is busy*
> *taking order.*

Woman a bosom a soft a fluthering flounces of bustle of.
Apron a, nice, not a mother, she like me sheila she'll she.
HEY take a nota me, nota bene, you're not looking, HEY
sheila lookamee he he HE.

> *Waitress smiles and talks to him.*

Ooh, who are you, a wonder a who aha, Who?

> *Second waitress brings soup for*
> *others.*

Where my foofare unfair I faint I fail you fail to feed me
FOUL FOUL where a waiter wanta waiter fillvoid waita
WAAAAA.

They give him more bread. He
throws it away crossly.

Filthy fare I fling it away. Never a fatherly fairshare.
Evera wanting waiting; baby delay be fatal. Rush proper
glugmurch, grubstew. Can't abear a wait a WAAAAA.

Meat course arrives and is cut
up for him. It is too hot.

Pssha, phthpta, I'm shot, struck, skewered in gullet. This
food got up an bit me.

He dreamily rubs potato over
the tray, his face.

Hole round world potato. Such stuff as dreams. Stuff a
potato. I'm a potato. I'm world. I'm potato. World is
potato. Indistinguish stufflines; no bounds, no forms,
Plato. Potato. Potation. HEY mad on a raft. WATER potation;
you're torturing, torture without water. WATER.

He is given water.

Gulp of St Torrents and All Sense; water. Guggle a bubble
involving uvula. Unparched, swallow a swillerby gurgle,
aaagh.

He suddenly wants to get down.

Unswaddle. Wanta toddle about, breakabound in a bun
dance. I'm become a regular wriggler, struggler to breaka-
bond. Lemme GO, confound your confining.

He sees they are embarrassed.

Scream an set the scene inauspicious, ennesspeecee, see?
Counterum a tantrum.

They pacify him with a sweet.

Lickalovely lumpish. Drool the goo goloptious. Lips a lovely.
Ah, the sugarmel, melting, sweetly saliva schlooping lovely
lovely.

NUITS BLANCHES 1964

10 p.m. After dinner in basic French hotel (air mild, dense, brackish; shiny old wooden spiral stairs, grey doors with straight handles, giant's-footsteps W.C., potatoey soup, beal or veef, hexagonal coffe cups, other guests all French except one morose English couple, wife wearing glasses, slacks, high heels), in small town reached after whole day bowling over forested ridges. Ask *patronne* what are big buildings above river. One is seminary, one home for old priests.

10.30 p.m. As usual, head too low on long bolster under bottom sheet, but too high on folded pillow – presumably must be folded, because 4 feet square. Why? They obviously know where human shoulder comes, they haven't got square bolster as well. Maybe it not pillow at all? Eiderdown for square child? Huge stomachwarmer, all French carry special tapes for tying warmer to their stomachs?

Own stomach unhappy about veef, or beal, or all those grapes. As though little men inside trying to lift heavy cover off well down which they want to pour something. Suddenly they manage it; *pripple-ipple-ipple gulLOY*, it runs into a kind of lake at bottom. But when turn over there seem to be other little men who want to pour it back again. Elsewhere pioneers digging new wells at right-angles (or blasting? Tiny muffled explosions). Parties of little men quarrelling (anti-bodies?), then uniting to blow up containing walls of several rivers, lakes, etc. Gurgling cataract rushes down smooth new channel, should be all right now; sense of release, peace in allegorical-symbolical landscape, in style of Dürer woodcut: *Das Land der Inner Man, trans-*

lated from ye German, London 1564. *With ye Mappe of Peris-taltia.* Peasant reclining by wide lake. But suddenly musket fire, *ping, gromp! Pripple ipple,* start again, lean cavalry scour plain, earthquake, smoke drifts across little low suns – *orblets,* anagram of bolster. Also *lobster, bolters, roblest* (*roblest Noman of them all*), *sterbol* (industrial detergent?), *bestrol* (pirate petrol firm) ...

Jerk awake. *Why* square pillow? Chuck it out, try to sleep again on bolster. *Or belts. Or blest.* Pak op *trobles* in ol kit bag ... Old priests nodding, smiling, long grey hair like Abbé Liszt, in front row of armchairs at Christmas play by seminarists, mumming Trojan War with wooden swords, but one seminarist, dressed as maid, answers telephone in rapid French which understand perfectly, for somehow it is English as well. Suddenly curtains fall, chairs turned over as old priests, seminarists, rush out to belfry and man ropes – 12 midnight. Old French hymn on bells in moonlit spire:

Bong, ting clang bong, clang,
Ting clang bong bing bang;
Bong, clang ting bong, clang,
Ting tong bing bong clang.

No, 19th-century hymn. Much more awake than in day-time now (ROT bels!), have super-consciousness of lacy Gothic 19th-cent. church, full of widows with pursed lips, Gothic bells in huge Dürer-Carolingian landscape, messages from Pope over forested ridges to Cologne, Rome, Aachen, Lindisfarne. Meanwhile 19th-cent. atheists riposte with monster town clock, strikes every hour *twice*. No tunes, just BUENGG, BUENNG. Fiery atheist-syndicalist 19th cent. mayor in tricolour sash, M. Alphonse Rataplan, unveiling municipal clock. Name of a name, is not pure time the measure of human progress, *mes amis*, rather than the tunes of an ignorant past? Ceremony boycotted by widows. Band of *sapeurs pompiers*, poum poum poum. Battle of the Bells. Dong clang bong ... *Gromp, pripple ipple* ...

Try folding pillow then. Where hell it? Grope. Crash. Tinkle. Damn. Knocked over glass of mineral water, specially put on floor in case huge pillow knocked it off bedside table. Lean firmly against pillow now foot high; perhaps French sleep sitting up …

1 a.m. *Bong Ting* hymn is played every hour.

2 a.m. How did municipal clock manage to strike *before* Bong Ting this time? Atheist mayor in red night-cap, cackling to himself, climbing up stairs in clock tower with lantern to advance it.

In silence after mighty tintinnabulation, tiny waspish noise, growing louder. It is mo-ped, coming in over lonely moonlit forested ridges. Stops next door to hotel. Huge iron gates creak open, animated conversation. Mo-ped starts up again, no silencer (ridden by Monsignor with urgent message for Rome, no time for repairs), *bwam bwam* off past snoring old priests, dreaming seminarists, lacy spire, into empty forest. What *was* message? Man next door now creaks gates open wider, starts up huge diesel lorry, shouts for helpers to load it with buckets, planks, bins, angle-iron, bellbuoys, crankcases, billboards, gongs, clang-pots, thundersheets. Urgent, driver impatiently revs up engine, finally roars off, gate creaks shut.

3 a.m. Entire performance repeated, although can't tell whether it is a new Monsignor or same one back from forest. What they *doing?* Resolve to look out of window next time, presumably 4 a.m., and see. Tie great pillow round head with luggage strap, both ears covered. Should probably have slept anyhow, anyway, next thing it is

8 a.m. All quiet as grave except for woman in dressing-gown taking down shutters opposite. Shall never know now.

THE RUSKIT ROUTES

All these roads of England from east to west are peaceful;
Sailing clouds float over the wheat, sun-gold in husk; it's
No good writing verse in a jerky metre – if I
Don't use these hexameters, well, verse sounds too brusque,
    it's
Lines like these I need for the van, near Cambridge, painted
PINJAR STUFFINGS, PEPPER AND SPICES, YEASTLESS
    RUSKITS.

Wondering drove I mile after mile behind this legend
Runic, rhythmic, hinting at foods with Fortnum prices,
Eastern, wine-cooked, eaten in calm St Neots or Bedford;
Peacock, *foie gras*, wonderful truffly things, weird ices –
No, but Brillat-Savarin stuff like this can't, surely,
Tempt these ploughmen calling for dumplings, scorning
    spices?
Toothless rustics mumping on yeastless riskits, maybe?
Could there be some hint of a local name in PINJAR?
Peppered Shepherd's pie, is it known through all these
    counties
(Laced with ginger, heard in the speech round here as
    jinjar)?

England-spanning A45, from Felixstowe to
Where in booming Birmingham B.S.A. make muskets,
Lured by signposts (Waterbeach, Woolpit, Offord d'Arcy)
Down your length I marvelled and mused on biscuits,
    ruskits,
Mystics, rustics, music, and names like Saffron Walden,

Mansions (Papworth Everard), churches, yews subfuse; it's
Here one finds the soul of the country, not where southbound,
Northbound, cars from London are jammed from dawn till
    dusk, it's
Here, in secret farms, little pubs with clapboard tarwashed;
Here, more strange than Araby faint with nard and musk,
    it's
Here, where long-lost villages fill far plains, and men eat
PINJAR STUFFINGS, PEPPER AND SPICES, YEASTLESS
    RUSKITS.

THEY LAUGHED WHEN ...

The elegant modern concert hall was packed. A rather insignificant-looking little man came on, bowing happily and nervously as the audience roared its applause. When it had died down he said, 'I should like – *goodness*, how I should like – to play you Chopin's *Première Ballade*'. He sat down at the beautiful Steinway, and then began the most fantastic public performance I have ever heard.

Technically the music was wildly beyond him; yet there was an extraordinary *rapport* between him and the audience, to whom he spoke in confidential asides, in the manner of Pachmann. At the very third bar of the quite simple opening statement in octaves, *largo*, his left hand began playing at an interval of a ninth instead of an octave. 'Damn, I always make that mistake', he said. When the great A major melody arrived, he first played the left hand alone, then the right, saying, 'then you get this glorious melody on top'. Cadenzas and chromatic runs he played *adagio* ('it goes like this, only faster'). The whole thing was a curious outline of this famous piece, like a giant's skeleton seen through bottle glass. He ended on a very loud (and for once correct) G minor chord.

The audience gave him a standing ovation. Afterwards, at a reception in his honour, I heard a lovely girl say, 'It wasn't only your playing, it was the insight of your remarks that gave me a new view of the music'.

My companion, a close-cropped, handsome woman in her early fifties, nodded approval. 'One of our easier successes', she said. 'This man's report showed he had a strain of brutal sarcasm, exercised increasingly on his wife and two children, threatening to break up the family. We found he was a frustrated pianist. A couple of weeks at this Admiration Centre will put him right. "They laughed when I sat down to play", as your English proverb has it; but here they *admire* him, as you've seen. He'll leave here all sweetness and light.'

The speaker was Dr Anna List, whose work as founder of the Admiration Centre movement is drawing social workers and penologists from all over the world. It has, of course, long been known that a great deal of crime and neurosis (to Dr List practically interchangeable terms, as they were in *Erewhon*) stems from the frustration of the universal desire to be admired. But until Dr List's pioneering work the attitude of society was a hopeless acceptance of the iron laws of heredity, environment and pure chance which make some people admirable and others not.

'There used to be a lot of truth,' she told me, 'in that joke about the psychiatrist who said to his patient, "My dear sir, I'm afraid I can't cure you. You haven't got a complex, you really *are* inferior". But we hope we are altering all that. Basically the secret lies in two things. The admiration must, of course, be genuine; and there must be specialisation.

'Let me tell you about the specialisation first. This particular Admiration Centre is, of course, for music – all kinds, instrumental and vocal. It has a permanent staff of 300 Admirers. There's a similar one for the plastic arts about a dozen miles from here; not such a large staff there, just enough to fill a biggish studio-cum-gallery.

'But most of the other thirty-seven are General Admiration Centres. Not everyone wants to be admired for anything so specific as playing the piano. Nevertheless there are three rough sub-divisions: Moral, Witty and Physical. These are the basic desires: to be admired because you are more generous, brave or honest than the Admirer; because you are more amusing, a gayer companion; or (for men) simply a better fighter with better muscles or (for women) more beautiful.

'Naturally these categories usually overlap. To be admired for being brave often involves both the Moral and the

Physical. Certain types of Witty admirees (as we call them) are proud of being *not* brave; and so on. Each case is different, but by now we have built up such a varied staff of Admirers that we can fit any individual, from the complex personality who wishes to be admired simultaneously as Moral, Witty and Physical to the simple, well-set up lad (I think we can claim to have saved hundreds of them from turning into petty thugs) who merely wants to show off his muscles. In his case our staff often have to let themselves be beaten up.'

'It sounds miraculous', I said. 'But where do you *get* your staff ?'

'Ah, that's the beauty of it – and they're all genuine Admirers', said Dr List, the light of the pioneer enthusiast in her eyes. 'The staff of Admirers are people who couldn't get a pass at any of our Centres. No matter how much they were praised, they still knew that they were so cowardly, un-witty, weedy, and so on, that they would never be any good. This makes their admiration genuine, but it does not sap their own self-respect, because in our country it is a great honour to be an official Admirer. Of course they get certain material privileges – they receive high salaries and pay no income tax – but most of all they, too, are admired as devoted public servants of a system that has emptied our prisons and is fast emptying our hospitals.'

I learned much more from Dr List; of the highly organised follow-up system – letters to admirees telling how their prowess is still remembered, the placing of laudatory reviews and news items; the special Travelling Admirers (our returned pianist, struggling with his Chopin again at home, might hear a knock on his door, a man with dark glasses on the doorstep would say, in a foreign accent, 'Blease to poddon me, I am walking down ze street and I am hearing zis *so* beautiful masterplaying ...'). I learnt of the ambitious plans to operate the scheme not only for individuals but for nations. 'Some whole countries', said Dr List with a twinkle, 'have dangerous inferiority complexes.' And I came away utterly convinced that this great woman has an idea which could save the world.

THE SAUCY BLACK MARIA

Surely one of the most inscrutable groups of men in London is the river police. Of course, *all* police have this odd, shut-away side, this private life of rank and hierarchy. They hold brief inspections, officers with black moustaches (there is a police moustache, different from both the Army and the R.A.F. varieties), carrying gloves, inspect rows of men at attention. There is no shouting or marking time, it is all done quickly, casually, behind some building, in some semi-private field when they think the public isn't looking.

Their uniforms indicate only the Shakespearean ranks – captain, sergeant, constable; you never hear of a police-major or a police-corporal, these suggest some Latin republic in the nineteenth century. There is something elusive about police rank. Is a police captain a real captain, with those chromium-looking stars?* It seems half-way between the real and the metaphorical, the Army and the Salvation Army.

But it is tremendously real to the police themselves, in that inward-looking side of their life (they do not hate us or love us, they are just different. They have marvellously con-fraternal meetings with foreign policemen; they don't feel different from *them* at all, even if they wear swords or pick their teeth or take bribes. They have the same moustaches. You couldn't have Interarm or Internav – look at the Nato squabbles – but Interpol has been working harmoniously for years). And it would be nice to think that the river police

* No. I've checked. He's a Chief Inspector.

are only a kind of internal function, that they don't actually arrest pirates or smugglers, or even look out for them, but simply bring this rank business to a secret and perfect conclusion, with police-commodores gravely, silently saluting a police-admiral, in a mysterious marine dance, on some hidden stretch of the river, Policeman's Reach.

Yet of course real action is instantly suggested by their boats, which embody an odd contrast between rakish lines, hinted-at-powerful engines – and a lot of varnish and glass, a super-structure that seems to be made of office partitions; enclosed, impersonal, a tiny police station on water. More often than not these boats seem to be moored, empty, locked-looking, near some jolly trippers' pier at some such place as Charing Cross.

Where have the occupants gone? One imagines impossible dialogues. *Head her a point to starb'd. Aye aye sir. Steady as she goes. We'll make a landfall at Charing Cross and head those scoundrels off.* Or one sees them, sunburnt, lean, carrying reports into Bow Street or Savile Row stations with a rolling gait, slightly envied by the pale land-policemen at their humdrum desks. Perhaps there are even river police shanties –

> I'll tell you a tale of Inspector Brown
> *Haul, haul away O!*
> He sailed the canal to Camden Town
> *Way, haul away O! etc.,*

But the fact is, one can't imagine the sort of crime that police deal with (as opposed to Customs men or Board of Trade officials) happening actually *on* the river. Surely it is all in mysterious buildings bordering it. The furtive figure in the fog, the shadows in the warehouse, the creaking steps, the hoarse whisper. *Here come liver policeymen. Open tlap door* (kersplash). *Good evening, Inspector. It's all up, Fan Tan, we've got your master. Van Klompers. So, Inspector?* LOOK OUT, SIR! ... all this seems to require ordinary land-policemen, in glittering capes, waiting under piers, softly blowing whistles at Wapping Stairs.

If, on the other hand, we are in Hammond Innes country,

spies escaping abroad in fast launches, surely there would be signals to the Nore, slim grey shapes would nose out from Chatham, it would be a job for the Navy. Unless, of course, these river police managed to head them up river. *I'll open her up when we get past Tilbury. Flat calm forecast. Get me to K5 in Antwerp in six hours, there's 50,000 Swiss francs for you. Ahoy there, I have a warrant for your arrest. Curses. Hard about. We'll give them the slip at Henley Lock, there's an Auster in the meadow ... Dash it, Henderson, what are all those Chinese fellers doin' in the club boathouse? ...*

But I had regretfully to dismiss all these fantasies and to think of the river police as just roaring up and down and looking inscrutable, when I saw with my own eyes the following message scrawled on a Martini advertisement at the Monument Tube Station:

SCOTT TO THE RIVER
RED-HEAD SEMI-COMA

I wish I'd been at Charing Cross when the river policemen, called from their bunks in some shed hidden under the bridge by a terse radio message *Scott B4*, dashed down the steps, whipped off tarpaulins and roared away. I hope they got to Red-head in time.

SCHILLER-SCHALLYING

I just have this feeling that I am going to get to the end of
my life without ever knowing about Schiller. I look at the
sodden January garden and see the bean poles still there,
indeed the ruined fruit net and even a deck chair, everything crying out *Get on with it, Jennings, keep the depreciation
down*; in the bank of life I am six months in the red.

I still hope, looking at my table of Books Being Read (or
at least Started) that one day I shall finish Mann's *Dr
Faustus*, the Hugo Italian Course, *Harmony*, by Walter Piston
and *Childe Harold's Pilgrimage*, to name but four. Everybody
else, or at least everybody else that writes those literary
reminiscences in *The Times*, seems to have read *Childe Harold*
at the age of 13 while the rain, gently unheard, drummed
on the attic roof of the old rambling house in Hampshire.
However. And what about this, for the Beatles?

> In sooth, it was no vulgar sight to see
> Their barbarous, yet their not indecent, glee;
> And as the flames along their faces gleamed,
> Their gestures nimble, dark eyes flashing free,
> The long wild locks that to their girdles streamed,
> While thus in concert they this lay half sang, half
>   screamed:
> Tambourgi! Tambourgi!* etc.

But somehow Schiller is in the same class as ski-ing for
me. I should love to be good at it, but it's too late now, even

* The Beatles' pressing of *Tambourgi* is already way up in the charts, and
like you can guess from the title, Ringo is great, man, and I mean fab. At
least, I think I do.

if I had the time or the money (same thing, in the bank of life). The virgin snowfields call to more fortunate, younger men. Other, more rounded minds than mine will have their grand vision of western culture completed by knowing this great, er, Romantic, er, author of, er – of course, I could look it all up in an encyclopedia but I'm damned if I will.

Even so, I can't *ignore* Schiller the way I am compelled to ignore, say, Lope de Vega, or this great Argentinian Jorge Borges (I think) or Anaxagoras (500–428 B.C.), all great and good men, I'm sure. I have this picture, doubtless wrong, of Schiller's astral body, large, pantheistic, diffuse, like a big smiling airship among green meadows, because of some Schubert songs I know and the Ode to Joy at the end of Beethoven's Choral Symphony.

I was actually singing in this a few weeks ago, because when I ought to be getting up the bean poles (or, before I know where I am, putting them back again; perhaps I'll just *leave* them now) I have the honour of singing in the Philharmonia Chorus. They don't ask you about Schiller at the audition, you just have to sing.

Like the rest of the singers in the Ninth, I was one of the audience until the last 20 minutes of this marvellous holy drunken work, so it's all right, I hope, for me to say that old unsmiling Klemperer opened heaven that night. For the first moment you think that controlled and objective beat of his is just an intellectual clock, and then suddenly you realize it isn't a clock at all, it's the tremendous heart of Beethoven himself beating.

Afterwards, back in the everyday analytical world, I found myself wondering how I could have sung in this performance (and another in 1947 under Sabata), and listened to the work scores of times, without knowing the actual meaning of the words so honoured by Beethoven – these verbal concepts emerging at the very end, a final statement, a paradisal island rising miraculously from the profound and stormy ocean of his symphonic life; all music aspiring to the condition of poetry, to reverse that saying of whoever it was.

Of course, like everyone else, I knew the famous bits.

Joy, *tochter aus Elysium*, daughter of Elysium. *Seid umschlungen, Millionen*, I embrace ye, Millions (*umschlungen*, sounds like a big shlooping kiss), *diesen Kuss der ganzen Welt*, this kiss to the whole world. But what about the bit the choir actually come in on:

> *Deine Zauber binden wieder*
> *Was die Mode streng getheilt*
> *Alle Menschen Werden Brüder*
> *Wo dein sanfter Flügel weilt.*

Zauber – ah, yes, magic (*Zauberflöte*, the Magic Flute). Then, before I could stop it –

> Your magic bindweed
> Which the Mode strongly something (recommends?)
> All men become brothers
> Where your something bird lives

Heavens, must exorcise this anti-climactic picture of the huge girl, Joy, in great modish Hat trimmed with bindweed with a bird in it, vast crowd of brothers in lederhosen all in love with her. Quick, look up translation given in the programme:

> Your magic reunites
> What custom sternly separated
> All men shall be brothers
> There where your gentle wings tarry

Of course. Very beautiful. (And that was a good guess about *Flügel*.) Now what about this line; it must be very important, we tenors have a most tremendous shout on it –

> *Ahnest du den Schöpfer, Welt?*

Utterly opaque except for *Welt* (world). *Ahnen*, what it mean? To own? That sounds a German-rooted word. Or perhaps some beautiful, untranslatable German concept, *invented* by Schiller perhaps, 'to say *Ah!* to, to worship, admire'? And *Schöpfer*? A chopper? What about this *pf* in it? *Pferd* is horse (oh, one knows the odd word), *schön* is beautiful. *Schön-pferd, schöpfer*?

Do you own the Chopper, World?
Do you say Ah! to the beautiful horse, World?

No good, look it up quick. Ha, yes:

Do you sense your Creator, World?

Indeed I do, and I sense Schiller too. You can sense *everything* in music.

UNDER MILK SHED

Birdsong burgeoning, wake from winterwoe. Dibble double-dig get orgardenized, summersoon seed-sown. Trickle a trench, perfection peas and beauty-broad beans, brandish bangfoil tinbright to botherbirds, ward 'em with wirework netfoil, blast 'em. Secateurs too, rosecut bushtrim for beauty-burst. Forkspade muck-spreading, wormatiller, wheremetools, get at it.

Tools in shed. Trust it tidy neatstack, racktools in regular rowform. Sharp shedshock! Angular jungle of mingled poleprops, pram-nets, pumps and paintcans, slidover lidoff lava solidified. Matter multiplies, interlockweave tangle. Jumble germinates from orgy in stables when no one looking. Props and poles proliferate, raketeeth racktooth bracketed. See, bicycle tricycle socketed interstices, pedalstuck in slidover spokes, sprocketstuckfast braketwist embracing handlemower mixmachine in medley of wirewheels!

AND whence polypaintpots, pigment augmented? What lotpots! Where gotpots, why? What dabbledaubing and bedizening from dozendizzy tintpots, lilacoliveoatmeal offwhite undercoat undertaken overestimated? *Quot* pots *tot* brushes in turpjar empty, stucktogether stickbristles. Posterpaint too, polychromatic powders purple-pink peagreen petunia (toddlertots paintpots, primary posterpaint primitive, Grandma mosesmess). Pint pot primer prise it open, ug, glugbottom treacletop. Stickstir stiffpaint stuckfast.

Stay, stop purposeless paintpottering! Clenchteeth clinch-it, cleanshed shirtsleeves, start somewhere. Shut paintpot, sharp tap to sealtop airseal, sludge will solidify else. Hammertap. Ho hum, where hellhammer? Tumbletoolbox a looselitter of latches and lampbits, jumblejunky loosebits uselessly roiled and rustridden, but where hellhammer? Ha, househidden. Howlhunt and family-fright, where hellhammer, who had it? Toldbefore not tampertoolbox, holy to headhouse. Where hellhammer?

Hedgehidden, half hour to find it (children chucked it).

Hammertap paintseal, blast it, bungle banglid, bashclang canister crashes to concrete, curse it, squirting gumsplodge and treaclepaint trousertips. Perishing poxpaint. Mop it up then, miles of mouldy material here, clutterclothes and ragrabble rumpled all smelly pellmell (*why*, whence winceyette pyjamapaints, woeful woolwaste ragtattiness, abandoned abundance? Memo, mustbincinerate, disembarrass).

Ha, freeflannel, filthyfeeling, only fit to paddle in puddlepaint. Fish it out – *faugh!* Full of furryfellows, weevils, woodlice wigglewormwalkers, favourite home in frostyfug winter, scuttle and skitter, spider skedaddles to seclusion. Bulb boxes beneath, bugsnug buried by battered dogblanket.

Damn, dahlias dead, dodo-dead, died in December doubtless, frost-finished. Precious-pretty priceplants perishable, can't preserve 'em professional (admen orderform, seedsmen send again, colour in catalogues, cheque cheque cheque). Apples hagshrunk too, horrible headshrunk coxbox. Only prosy potato lifebursting, tuber *mirabilis* pullulating tendriltwists in Aprildark, feelerblind a groping poking edwards.

COME, continue perseverance in clearance, weeding and seeding must wait, can't start from shambleshed. Cleanse in a frenzy. Surely September shed was shipshape, not sleazy slovenslum? Whence bulky bagboxes, crustycardboard cluttercrates (Christmas?). Kick 'em, curse cartons (toecap catchrake and catch a kneecap). Whence unstackable sticks and stakes stuckfast in stockpile, linked with line lengths, Laocöonhose turned and twisted?

Get 'em out, deckchair, bicycle stickrods hosepipe dogblanket lugchair gardenseat teakweight luglegs come on yer dadblasted dogblanket blankety hellhole, what hell holding it, *corm* on yer, wrench it tugleg higgledypiggledy. *Clank-dang*! Chaoscrash! Topple of toolbox, nailscatter, fiddling and finicky fingerfeeling for nuts and tiny tintacks.

Tryagain tugleg, pullpole and wanglewire. Bicycle balance broken, bangleg crankbracket, crackbang on shinbone.

Tryagain, tiptoe wrestle to slip hoseloop off beanpole in rafterpile (*how* hoselooped, who lassoo'd trestle?). Polepile pellmell, sledge dislodged (also rafterstacked afterthought) clonk dong clang ...

Summersoon seedsown, must get on startseason. Spring shedblossom, autumn shedleaves, but allyear shedshambles.

PHEASANT DREAMS

Whenever I look at cows or pheasants I always feel that Sartre and the boys are wrong to say that 'existence precedes essence', that man first exists, arbitrarily, *absurdly*, and all attempts to find or create any absolute rational or moral order, to reason about *what* man is, come afterwards, too late. Now suppose man were cow. There's a boring life for you; nothing but munch munch, milk milk, men with sticks yelling *gurmon yer*, *GROO yer*, your head always getting stuck under wire fences, only able to make this one sound, *murURM*; no chance of cow-kind evolving, getting rid of some of those four stomachs, growing thumbs on the forelegs and learning to handle tools with them, to write, draw, play the piano, because actually man controls the evolution of cows, making them ever less articulated and athletic, ever more just great artificial sacks of milk slung between insecure legs with bony knees.

All this about the Absurd – surely it would be much *more* Absurd to be a cow. I am sure it is part of some tremendous Plan that I am not a cow.

It's rather different with pheasants. At least cows don't know they are cows, they have never thought about it. But pheasants, like all birds only more so, have thought about it *and got it wrong*, at least from our point of view. This is partly because they have those round, beady eyes on each side of their heads. It must be, then, that they can see all round them, and are therefore not so definite about where to go as man is. It's all right for man: he knows that the roughly oval-shaped landscape in front of him, framed by darkness at the back, sides, top and underneath – a solid darkness of bone,

skull, brain, being, *him*, at a concentrated, definite point –
is the landscape he is entering; that is where he is going
(unless of course he turns round).

But if pheasants have this all-round vision, if they can see
behind them, an element of ambiguity is immediately intro-
duced. They might just as well go the other way. And why
does one have this obscure feeling that the air displaced in
going forward, particularly *flying* forward, would induce in
any creature with such vision an exposed draughty feeling
at the back of the head, where it should be all dark, closed
in, secret?

However, that is not the end of the complication in a
pheasant's *Weltanschauung*. Although its eyes can see all
round horizontally, it must be remembered that the top of
its head comes between them; the pheasant can't see all the
sky as well. It must have this all-round vision, but with a
circle of darkness above. Then of course there would be the
darkness framing the bottom edge of its vision, as with us;
so the pheasant could never really be sure which of these
darknesses contained *it* – the saucer-shaped darkness above
its eyes, above this 360 – deg. panoramic vision, or the dark
underneath. And surely this would give any pheasant an odd
feeling that it is two pheasants.

The curious thing is that *I* am beginning to think that every
pheasant is two pheasants, and so does everyone else who has
been twenty miles outside London in the past year. There
are more and more pheasants, clanking about in ditches,
walking along roads, rising in that cumbrous, flapping, ptero-
dactyl fashion of theirs (this is because they are not really
sure whether they are rising or falling, perhaps that dark bit
above their heads is the earth). They have no idea that men
are shooting them (although in a dim way they know I haven't
got a gun; don't worry about *him*, they say); they just know
that there are certain places where their friends get heart-
attacks and fall (or rise) without a word of warning, and
that those ditches and roads, and my garden, are not such
places.

Yesterday two very fat ones, who looked to me as if they

were called Frumper and Trudgetts, were walking gravely among my cabbages, trying to sort it all out.

'How many of us are there, Frumper?'

'Do you mean how many of *you*, Trudgetts? Why, you're Trudgetts and I'm the Frumpers' (a pheasant thinks *it* is two, but, naturally, any other pheasant looks like one pheasant to it).

'Why don't you say, "we're the Frumpers", Frumper?'

'How do you mean? You're not a Frumper, Trudgetts.'

'No, no, of course not; but you can't say "I'm the Frumpers", or rather *you're* the Frumpers. You'd have to say "we", but excluding me.'

'So I should hope. You're Trudgetts.'

'Yes, we're the Trudgetts, I see that –'

'Oh, nonsense. I've told you, we're *Frumpers*; you must say "I'm Trudgetts".'

'What do you mean, "Frumpers"? My dear Frumper, don't you see ...'

Goodness, it would be almost better to be a cow. But how much better to be us. Let's not hand the whole thing over to them.

PIANOLESCENCE

I discovered with rage recently that my piano had become obsolete. I had always thought that pianos were among the few things that don't do this. You don't read about tests by Our Piano Correspondent of some new model in which 'all the black notes are grouped conveniently together under the player's eye', or the casters have overdrive, or a remote-control device enables you to carry the lightweight plastic keyboard from room to room. This year's two-tone finish (sharp and flat) is the same, I had assumed, as last year's, and last century's.

A 7-octave-plus piano (mine has 88 notes) is, essentially, a combination of a harp (upright or, in the case of a boudoir grand like mine, lying down, naturally) and 88 lunatic mousetraps, or escapements from a wooden clock, or Leonardo da Vinci models illustrating the articulation of the human arm, used in medical lectures at Bologna in the sixteenth century. They are probably made of fragile, nearly extinct woods, of felt from the hides of small and increasingly rare animals found in the Carpathians, and unobtainable old Belgian glues.

Obsolescence is not simply a matter of tuning. However well one keeps it tuned, after a time the military regularity of those rows of hammers, which make the inside of a piano being played look like a tiny gymnastic display of little men rhythmically nodding and jumping and running, goes irretrievably slack. Three adjacent notes somewhere in the middle range sound a mournful twangling *wee-owng* that goes on for some time after one has finished playing. At a later stage, more notes go *wee-owng*, then they all do. One white note sticks a little below the level of the rest. The pedal begins to squeak.

This may not happen if you have, say, a Blüthner, and special Blüthner men come round to your centrally-heated London house at regular intervals. But only one wall, on which a damp patch shaped like Australia appears every time it is misty, let alone when it rains, separates our piano from a wet field full of beet, fading off into foggy marshes and the creeping sea. In gold letters on the lid it says FRANZ LIEHR, LIEGNITZ, SPECIAL ROYAL APPOINTMENT, with a very synthetic-looking coat of arms.

I am pretty sure there aren't any special Liehr men, and if there are I bet they don't come right out here. In fact I shouldn't imagine there are many Liehr *pianos* now (nobody has ever said to me 'Ah, I see you have a Liehr'); probably that Special Royal Appointment changed the maker's life.

One sees the young Herr Liehr and his workmen, carrying the oblong racks and legs into which all pianos disintegrate so easily at the turn of a few squeaky wooden pegs, ringing the bell of the Schloss Bad-Schuhschein, its baroque onion domes gleaming in the timeless (well, nineteenth-century) sun.

The great iron-studded door is opened by the major-domo, to whom Liehr says 'Kindly to inform Her Illustriousness, the Gräfin von Bad-Schuhschein und Liegnitz, that I, Herr Liehr, the piano for her boudoir brought have'.

They all clump up the stairs to the turret boudoir. Deftly the workmen assemble the piano and withdraw. Liehr kisses the hand of the Gräfin, a raving dark-haired beauty (her mother was a Dentisti, from a minor branch of the Medici). 'So, *mein liebchen*, we succeeded', she says.

'Yes, Illustriousness.'

'Liebchen, why do you so coldly speak?'

'Why all these two years have you to me a letter never written?'

'Ach! My father watch me every day. I have so unhappy been!'

'Liebchen, Matilda, forgive me. Do not to weep. But now I am here, and your Herr Father is away, let us –'

'But first please, to play me a meisterwerk von Ludwig van Beethoven.'

Liehr plays the Hammerklavier Sonata brilliantly. He stares out of the boudoir window, over the neat villages of the Schuhschein valley to the peaks of the distant Katspitz, dazzling in the afternoon sun, then turns to the Gräfin. 'Yet your Herr Father would rather you married a mechanic, a maker of pianos, than one who plays them. Two years at the Nachtschule I was learning those *verdammte* hammers how to fit. . . .'

How it got from there to Barkers I can't imagine.

But when I bought it it was as good as new, with a beautiful sweet tone (it still has). Now, three notes go *wee-owng*, one goes *phlp*, and one just goes   ; this is apart, or perhaps not apart, from the fact that the keyboard is full of halfpennies and old tickets which various children have put down between the notes.

Actually it was I who did the note that goes   ; it used to go *wee-owng* and it seemed to me that the hammer simply wasn't hitting squarely. When I tried to bend it gently I found that you can't do this in a piano, all those fiddling little things are absolutely rigid and brittle, and of course it snapped off.

Naturally this was a challenge to my friend Harblow, who cherishes the illusion that any actual piece of *mechanism* will yield up its secrets to a rational man. Before I could think how to stop him he was whipping out those oblong racks. He recovered $1/2\frac{1}{2}$ from in between the keys and tied up the broken hammer with thread. He even vacuumed it, for it was full of that special piano dust. We put the racks back (why is a piano so heavy when they are all so light?); and now when I play that note it just goes   . I shall *have* to find a Liehr man now.

BY RAIL, WAKING

After years on aeroplanes, had almost forgotten that secret of Continental (Milan-Calais) train journey is to relax. At start (5.30 p.m.) no one in right compartment, corridors swarming with opera Chorus of Brigands. Village Women, Cigarette Workers, Soldiers, Parties of Scottish Youth, all clambering blindly over each other like ants, loaded with great bags and bundles (eggs?). Peevish English voice reiterates endlessly *but this one* IS 32. Official who organises *couchettes* doesn't even get on train till Lugano. (Or Lucerne, say some. Or Basle, say others.)

Relax, be old travellers, go to dining car. Sure enough, after great vealy meal, walk back through empty corridors. Where all Brigands, etc., *gone*? Train has stopped once or twice at small stations in high, remote, windy part of Switzerland – they can't all have got out here? (Burghers in nightcaps roused by shouting and wailing in streets, emergency clocken-glockenbell signals, blankets, soup, army cots in Town Hall . . .)

Find *couchette* man (why he's French, already! It's the railway that dissolves frontiers, not the aeroplane, which is really just a Bath Road cocktail bar that happens to be able to do 500 m.p.h., leaving you totally unprepared for mad foreign soldiers and money.) Find own *couchette*, relieved to find other couple not Brigands, but like us, got children, late cheap holiday, don't like go in same aeroplane. He jolly smiling Italian antique dealer.

Settle down, wives in lower bunks, men in upper. Antique dealer goes out to corridor, reappears magically 30 seconds later wearing pyjamas; have feeling he just pulled ripcord and joke suit fell off. All settle down, lights out. Well, if he pyjamas, me too. Terrible contortions under blanket (silly really, since dark anyway). Sit cross-legged trying to make place on rack for shoes. What hell this, ah yes, great bottle mineral water (remembered last time in *couchette*, waking with fearful thirst). Just shove it up a bi——*thub*! Bottle falls on tender inside of kneecap. Rub ferociously to relieve both pain and frustration at not being able to utter dreadful curses above whisper.

Not five minutes since lights out yet, antique dealer already snoring; regular, business-like snoring of man who means to snore for 10 hours. He has lots of hangers, even his shirt on a hanger (mine stuffed between shoes and string bag out of which great bottle fell). Hour after hour he snore, hangers clink gently as train rushes round bends so it can have long stop where snoring even more inescapable. Why? What they *doing?* Driver having great French soup, bread, wine, veal, in engine shed, while loudspeakers on windy platform appear to address political meeting (during nightwork porters' lunch hour, as it were), till railway gendarmerie break it up, charging with armoured trolleys. Tremendous doorslamming, shouts, *pheep-pheeps*. Then absolute silence. Except for damned antique dealer, *hornk, oik, hornk, oik*.

Why I only one kept awake by him (wives both asleep long ago)? What good his fool hangers, elegant luggage, what good if he have *trouser-press*, if he snore like Brigand? If he rich antique dealer, bought all those shirts and hangers, why not anti-snore operation, removal adenoids or something? Why he so *peaceful* about it? Snorers encountered in Army, etc., have always worked to crescendo ending in paroxysm, they wake up just in time to stop their entire mouth and tongue falling down into their lungs, then mumblegroan to comparative silence in which they can try to get to sleep before they start again. But antique dealer's snoring *is* his breathing, not a blemish on it.

Have read somewhere that short, sharp sound, e.g. whistle, will stop snorer. Whistle has open-air sound, like calling taxi,

sounds mad in hot dark snore-thundering compartment.
Rapid interrogative Italian from antique dealer's wife. He just
go on snoring. Lie utterly still, till she asleep again.

Will train ever start again? All gone away now, driver too.
Mind wanders. Going to be here for ever. Man isn't snoring
really (else wives would surely be awake too?), it is noise in
own head. What Italian for *snore*? French? *Ronfler, gonfler,*
please snore my tyres. Rhonchus, bronchus, man has rhon-
chitis. Roncesvalles, Valley of Snoring, awful rail limbo, we
here for ever. Stertor (Greek hero, dragon?).

Suddenly, unheralded, train lurches off again. Ha, idea.
Use coat as pillow, press *couchette* pillow over ear. By pressing
really hard and humming to self can shut out sound of snore;
but woken from light quarter-sleep by feeling *couchette* pillow
falling off the moment pressure relaxed. Snatch at it, in doing
so dislodge one, possibly two, of those hangers. Lie utterly
rigid again, imagining soft clothy rain of shirts, tousers, etc.,
floating down in darkness on to antique dealer's wife, lights
on, questions (at least it would wake snorer) – but no sound.
I only person awake in whole train. Going mad in dark.
Lunatic ornamentation of original idea, will *tie* pillow and
coat on either side of head, like enormous cloth headphones,
with luggage strap; *must* shut out snoring with which hot dark
claustrophobic universe now filled. Scrabble in rack for strap,
pull it off bag, wrench, tug, *thub*! Blasted bottle falls on
identical place, inside of kneecap. Dreadful pain, kneecap now
centre of dark universe, bright painburst with rays shooting
out. Read somewhere damage to kneecap dangerous; probably lame, huge spreading bruise, water on knee. *Mineral*
water on knee, mirthless joke in mad darkness ...

Morning, nodding and smiling over coffee at antique dealer
and wife, *couchettes* folded up, perfectly normal train journey
past many French brickworks and thin little woods. He asks
if I slept well, is obviously nice man. But next time will try
either to share with Brigands or go in two aeroplanes.

SIT STILL, THERE

THERE is really only one class of people
Whom I'd like to push off a very high steeple,
Whom I'd wish to get caught in textile machinery
Or baked to death in a Heinz baked beanery;
All sendable plagues I would willingly send
ON PEOPLE WHO LEAVE BEFORE THE END.
They creak up aisles in the midst of finales,
After coat-strugglings, bag-clickings, whispered parleys,
They kick your gloves as they scramble past
Just when the heroine breathes her last.
Are their horrible homes so far away
That the 9.28's the last train today?
Are they rushing away to a sale at Grantham
Or can't they abide the National Anthem?
Where are they going, with self-importance
That scorns politeness's Oughts and Oughtn'ts?

But why go on? For I cannot expect
This fine moral poem to have an effect
Since none of the people for whom it is penned
Will be decent enough to read to

THE END

Bill Tidy
FOSDYKE SAGA: TWELVE

Thelwell
ANGELS ON HORSEBACK
THELWELL'S GYMKHANA
PENELOPE
THELWELL COUNTRY
A LEG AT EACH CORNER
THELWELL'S RIDING ACADEMY
UP THE GARDEN PATH
THE COMPLEAT TANGLER
THELWELL'S BOOK OF LEISURE
THIS DESIRABLE PLOT
TOP DOG
THREE SHEETS IN THE WIND
BELT UP
THE EFFLUENT SOCIETY
THELWELL GOES WEST
THELWELL'S BRAT RACE

*Other humorous and diverting books
in Methuen Paperbacks*

Kenneth Baker (editor)
I HAVE NO GUN BUT I CAN SPIT

Lisa Birnbach
THE OFFICIAL PREPPY HANDBOOK

Arthur Block
MURPHY'S LAW VOL I
MURPHY'S LAW VOL II
MORE MURPHY'S LAW

Eleanor Bron
LIFE AND OTHER PUNCTURES

Sandra Boynton
CHOCOLATE: THE CONSUMING PASSION

Jilly Cooper
SUPER MEN AND SUPER WOMEN
WORK AND WEDLOCK

Graeme Garden
THE SEVENTH MAN

Frank Muir and Patrick Campbell
CALL MY BLUFF

Frank Muir and Denis Norden
THE 'MY WORD!' STORIES
TAKE MY WORD FOR IT!
OH MY WORD!

Bill Oddie
BILL ODDIE'S LITTLE BLACK BIRD BOOK

Katharine Whitehorn
WHITEHORN'S SOCIAL SURVIVAL
HOW TO SURVIVE IN HOSPITAL
HOW TO SURVIVE CHILDREN
HOW TO SURVIVE IN THE KITCHEN